FRIEDRICH NIETZSCHE

HERALD OF A NEW ERA

Friedrich Nietzsche

Herald of a New Era

William Bowman

Hazar Press

Friedrich Nietzsche: Herald of a New Era
William Bowman

Hazar Press

ISBN-13: 978-0997570304
ISBN-10: 099757030X

CONTENTS

PREFACE

When I was a young teenager, I was admitted to the hospital because I could not walk without excruciating pain in my legs. After two miserable weeks of counterproductive treatment, my doctor finally diagnosed my illness properly and prescribed the appropriate treatment. I remained another two weeks in the hospital. During an emotional low point, I saw G. Gordon Liddy on the television being released from prison after serving time for his role in the Watergate scandal. In response to reporters' questions, he said, "Was mich nicht umbringt, macht mich stärker." It was reported to be a quote from Friedrich Nietzsche meaning: "What does not kill me, makes me stronger." My father suggested that I think about that quote. I did. Shortly thereafter, I began to read Nietzsche's works. He taught me to think. Nietzsche is my educator. This book is the product of a lifetime of studying Nietzsche's works and thinking about what his ideas mean to us today.

William Bowman
Sils-Maria
June 2016

A NOTE ON CITATIONS

Nietzsche's works are cited in the endnotes according to the key below. Arabic numerals refer to sections, which are the same in all editions. For example, "GS, §341" means *The Gay Science*, section 341. For Nietzsche's books that are divided into essays, volumes, parts, or chapters, Roman numerals refer to such divisions. For example, "TI I, §8" means *Twilight of the Idols*, chapter 1, section 8.

A – *The Anti-Christ*
BGE – *Beyond Good and Evil*
BT – *The Birth of Tragedy*
CW – *The Case of Wagner*
D – *Daybreak*
EH – *Ecce Homo* (four parts [not numbered by Nietzsche] with sub-parts on Nietzsche's earlier works after part III)
    EH, Preface (including the epigraph on the page between the Preface and EH I)
    EH I – Why I Am So Wise
    EH II – Why I Am So Clever
    EH III – Why I Write Such Good Books
    EH-BT, EH-UM, EH-HA, EH-D, EH-GS, EH-Z, EH-BGE, EH-GM, EH-TI, EH-CW
    EH IV – Why I Am a Destiny
GM – *On the Genealogy of Morals* (three essays)
GS – *The Gay Science*
HA – *Human, All Too Human* (two volumes with two parts in the second volume)
    HA I – Volume I
    HA II1 – Volume II, part 1: Assorted Opinions and Maxims
    HA II2 – Volume II, part 2: The Wanderer and his Shadow
NW – *Nietzsche contra Wagner*
TI – *Twilight of the Idols* (eleven chapters [not numbered by Nietzsche])
    TI, Foreword
    TI I – Maxims and Arrows
    TI II – The Problem of Socrates

TI III – "Reason" in Philosophy
TI IV – How the "Real World" at last Became a Myth
TI V – Morality as Anti-Nature
TI VI – The Four Great Errors
TI VII – The "Improvers" of Mankind
TI VIII – What the Germans Lack
TI IX – Expeditions of an Untimely Man
TI X – What I Owe to the Ancients
TI XI – The Hammer Speaks
UM – *Untimely Meditations* (four essays)
UM I – David Strauss, the Confessor and the Writer
UM II – On the Uses and Disadvantages of History for Life
UM III – Schopenhauer as Educator
UM IV – Richard Wagner in Bayreuth
WLN – *Writings from the Late Notebooks* (a selection from Nietzsche's notebooks of the years 1885 through 1888 organized by notebook number followed by note number in brackets)
WP – *The Will to Power* (a selection from Nietzsche's notebooks of the years 1883 through 1888 published by Nietzsche's sister)
Z – *Thus Spoke Zarathustra* (four parts with individually entitled sections [not numbered by Nietzsche] and numbered subsections)

Dates in parentheses after book titles are original publication dates unless otherwise noted. Within quotations, ellipses in brackets are my omissions. Likewise, words in brackets are my additions. Ellipses without brackets are in the original.

I quoted extensively from Nietzsche's works for three reasons. First, a book in a foreign language already loses some of its original meaning when translated, but it loses even more if summarized or paraphrased. Second, quotations allow the reader to act as quality control of the quoted material and the context in which it is used. For this reason, the standard translations of Nietzsche's works are used unless otherwise noted. For the reader's convenience, an index of Nietzsche's works quoted or cited herein is provided at the end of the book. Third, Nietzsche was a brilliant writer. It would be a great disservice to the reader if Nietzsche's own words were not used as often as possible.

CHRONOLOGY

1844

Friedrich Wilhelm Nietzsche was born on 15 October 1844 in the tiny village of Röcken near Lützen, about twenty kilometers southwest of Leipzig, in the Prussian province of Saxony, the Lutheran heartland of Germany. He was born in the Röcken parsonage because his father, Carl Ludwig Nietzsche (1813-1849), was the parish pastor. Both of Nietzsche's grandfathers were also Lutheran pastors. His father was thirty-one years old and his mother, Franziska Oehler (1826-1897), was eighteen at the time of his birth. Because 15 October was also the birthday of the reigning Prussian king, Friedrich Wilhelm IV, Nietzsche's parents named him Friedrich Wilhelm in honor of their sovereign. In *Ecce Homo*, Nietzsche noted, "There was at least one advantage to the choice of this day: my birthday was a holiday throughout my childhood."[1] To his family and close friends, he was known as Fritz throughout his life. By the time of the publication of his first book in 1872, Nietzsche had dropped Wilhelm from his name.

1850

Nietzsche's father died of a brain disease in 1849 at the age of thirty-five and in early 1850 Nietzsche's younger brother died shortly before his second birthday. In the spring of 1850, Nietzsche moved about twenty-five kilometers southwest to Naumburg an der Saale ("on the Saale" river) at the age of five with his mother and younger sister, Elisabeth.

1858

After two temporary residences, Nietzsche and his family moved into house number 18 on Weingarten Street next to Naumburg's old city wall in the fall of 1858. Because of Nietzsche's scholastic achievements, the rector of the Pforta boarding school near Naumburg offered him free admission to what was considered the finest preparatory school for classical studies in Germany. Nietzsche entered this prestigious school in October 1858.

1864

Nietzsche graduated from Pforta in September 1864 and then attended university in Bonn. He was attracted to Bonn by its two leading philologists, Otto Jahn and Friedrich Ritschl. Initially studying theology, Nietzsche changed to philology after the first semester. At home for Easter, he told his mother that he would not follow his father into the Lutheran ministry. Nietzsche even refused to accompany her to the customary Easter church service. As he later explained, he never, "not even as a child," devoted any attention or time to the concepts "God," "immortality of the soul," "redemption," or "beyond." He was not an atheist as a result of any specific event in his life nor did he experience a crisis of faith. He claimed to be an atheist by "instinct." Nietzsche was "too inquisitive, too *questionable*, too exuberant to stand for any gross answer. God is a gross answer, an indelicacy against us thinkers – at bottom merely a gross prohibition for us: you shall not think!"[2]

1865

After one year in Bonn, Nietzsche decided to pursue his philological studies in Leipzig where Professor Ritschl had accepted a position and was about to commence teaching. Nietzsche arrived in Leipzig in October 1865, a couple of days after his twenty-first birthday. His discovery of Arthur Schopenhauer's *The World as Will and Representation* during his first semester had a profound influence on him.

1867

In October 1867, Nietzsche reported for duty to a field artillery regiment in Naumburg to fulfill his compulsory military service. He was injured while horseback riding in March of the following year, which resulted in his spending the remainder of his military service as a convalescent. On his twenty-fourth birthday in 1868, Nietzsche's military service expired. Shortly afterward, he returned to Leipzig to continue his studies.

1868

Because of his talented piano-playing skills and keen interest in the musical works of Richard Wagner, Nietzsche was invited to a small gathering at Wagner's sister's house in Leipzig to meet the famous composer in November 1868. The fifty-five-year-old composer was so impressed by the young student that he invited Nietzsche to visit him at his home in Switzerland so they could continue their discussions about music and the philosophy of Schopenhauer, two topics for which they were both enthusiastic.

1869

Based on his essays in a philological journal and a very strong recommendation by Professor Ritschl, Nietzsche was appointed as professor extraordinarius (i.e., without tenure) of classical philology at the University of Basel in Switzerland in February 1869 without being required to pass the normal final examinations or complete a doctoral dissertation at Leipzig. The twenty-four-year-old Nietzsche arrived in Basel in April. In order to take the position, he renounced his Prussian citizenship, but he never completed the process to become a Swiss citizen. After one year of teaching, Nietzsche was appointed professor ordinarius (i.e., with tenure).

Basel was within easy train distance of Wagner's lake-side house in Tribschen near Lucerne. Nietzsche visited Wagner at Tribschen for the first time in May 1869. Over the next three years – until Wagner moved to Bayreuth in April 1872 – Nietzsche made twenty-three visits to Tribschen. Nietzsche called his "intimate relationship" with Wagner "by far the most profound and cordial recreation of my life."

> I'd let go cheap the whole rest of my human relationships; I should not want to give away out of my life at any price the days of Tribschen – days of trust, of cheerfulness, of sublime accidents, of *profound* moments. I do not know what experiences others have had with Wagner: *our* sky was never darkened by a single cloud.[3]

1872

Die Geburt der Tragödie aus dem Geiste der Musik (The Birth of Tragedy out of the Spirit of Music) was Nietzsche's first book. He was twenty-seven years old when it was published in January 1872. Although Nietzsche dedicated *The Birth of Tragedy* to Richard Wagner,[4] he later admitted that the book's "practical application to Wagnerism, as if that were a symptom of *ascent*," was wrong.[5]

Writing during the "exciting time"[6] of the Franco-Prussian War of 1870-1871, Nietzsche began *The Birth of Tragedy* "amid the thunder of the battle of Wörth,"[7] which occurred on 6 August 1870, as he "sat somewhere in an Alpine nook, very bemused and beriddled, hence very concerned and yet unconcerned, and wrote down his thoughts about the *Greeks*."[8] Two days later, Nietzsche requested a temporary leave of absence from his teaching duties in order to make whatever contribution he could to his Fatherland's war effort. Basel's education board granted the request, provided that Nietzsche restricts his participation in the war to medical care of the wounded. He immediately traveled to Lindau, Germany, and joined an auxiliary medical unit as a "medical orderly." Following the victorious German army into France, he eventually found himself on duty before the walls of the besieged French city of Metz on cold September nights, still thinking about the Greeks.[9] Shortly thereafter, Nietzsche became sick with dysentery and diphtheria while caring for wounded soldiers with the same ailments. When he was well enough to travel, he was discharged and traveled to Naumburg on 19 September to convalesce. He returned to Basel shortly after his twenty-sixth birthday. Nietzsche completed the final draft of *The Birth of Tragedy* in the spring of 1871 while he was still "slowly convalescing from an illness contracted at the front."[10]

1873-1876

While still a professor in Basel, Nietzsche completed four out of a planned thirteen essays on the state of contemporary German culture. Although he called them *Unzeitgemässe Betrachtungen* (*Untimely Meditations*), they were anything but untimely. Each essay was published separately over a three-year period. *David Strauss der Bekenner und der Schriftsteller* (*David Strauss, the Confessor and the Writer*) was published in August 1873; *Vom Nutzen and Nachtheil der Historie für das Leben* (*On the Uses and Disadvantages of History for Life*) in February 1874; *Schopenhauer als Erzieher* (*Schopenhauer as Educator*) in October 1874; and *Richard Wagner in Bayreuth* (*Richard Wagner in Bayreuth*) in July 1876, the year in which the Bayreuth opera house was opened and the month before the first public performance of *The Ring of the Nibelung*, which inaugurated Wagner's Bayreuth Festival. The four essays were not published again until 1893 when they were compiled in one book.

1878

Appearing in May 1878, *Menschliches, Allzumenschliches: Ein Buch für freie Geister* (*Human, All Too Human: A Book for Free Spirits*) was Nietzsche's first book of aphorisms. He dedicated the first edition to the memory of Voltaire, "a *grandseigneur* ["nobleman"] of the spirit – like me,"[11] in commemoration of the hundredth anniversary of the French philosopher's death on 30 May 1778.

Nietzsche began *Human, All Too Human* immediately after the inauguration of the Bayreuth Festival in August 1876, but he wrote the majority of the book between October 1876 and May 1877 while he was on sabbatical in Sorrento, Italy, on the coast south of Naples. While the Wagners were staying in a nearby hotel, Nietzsche met Richard Wagner for the last time before the Wagners departed for Rome in early November 1876. After returning to Basel in September 1877 to resume his teaching duties, Nietzsche completed the book during the winter of 1877-1878.[12]

Although the intellectual break with Wagner came almost two years earlier,[13] the final break in the friendship with Wagner came in 1878 after the exchange of Wagner's *Parsifal* and Nietzsche's *Human, All Too Human* in the mail. "This crossing of the two books – I felt as if I heard an ominous sound – as if two swords had crossed. – At any rate, both of us felt that way; for both of us remained silent."[14] After Wagner had sent a copy of the libretto of *Parsifal* to Nietzsche in January 1878, Nietzsche mailed a copy of *Human, All Too Human* to Wagner in April 1878.

Nietzsche completed *Vermischte Meinungen und Sprüche* (*Assorted Opinions and Maxims*) at the end of 1878. It was published in March 1879 as an "Appendix" to *Human, All Too Human.*

1879

In *Ecce Homo*, Nietzsche wrote that in 1879 at age thirty-six (about the same age at which his father died), "I reached the lowest point of my vitality – I still lived, but without being able to see three steps ahead."[15] His worsening eyesight and continuing bouts of migraine headaches accompanied by nausea and paroxysmal seizures (from 1873 until three months before his loss of sanity, Nietzsche was never free of these problems for more than a few weeks at a time) forced him to resign from his professorship in May 1879 after only ten years. With a small pension from the university, Nietzsche could now continue writing without worrying about earning an income.

Both the break with Wagner and the resignation from his professorship were emancipating events for Nietzsche. He was now free to write without the burden of Wagner's friendship or teaching duties.

Nietzsche spent the summer in St. Moritz, Switzerland, where he wrote *Der Wanderer und sein Schatten* (*The Wanderer and his Shadow*). It was published in December 1879 as the "Second and Final Supplement" to *Human, All Too Human*.

1881

Nietzsche's next book of aphorisms, *Morgenröthe: Gedanken über die moralischen Vorurtheile* (*Daybreak: Thoughts on the Prejudices of Morality*), was published in July 1881. Nietzsche began *Daybreak* in February 1880 in Riva on Lake Garda in northern Italy and then continued writing as he traveled throughout the year to Venice, Marienbad in Bohemia, Naumburg, Stresa on Lake Maggiore, and finally Genoa, where he completed the book in early 1881.

1882

Nietzsche's last book of aphorisms, *Die fröhliche Wissenschaft* (*The Gay Science*), was published in August 1882. He started the book in July 1881 during his first summer in Sils-Maria, a small village in the Upper Engadine region of Switzerland, where he stayed in a rented room above a grocery in a simple, two-story house. He returned to stay in this same room during every summer from 1883 to 1888.

From October 1881 to March 1882, Nietzsche continued writing in Genoa, where he spent "the most wonderful month of January I ever experienced."[16] He completed the book in Messina, Sicily, in April 1882. With *The Gay Science*, Nietzsche ended six years (1876-1882) of "*Freigeisterei*" ("free-spiriting") that began with *Human, All Too Human*.

Nietzsche spent the summer of 1882 in Tautenburg about twenty-two kilometers southwest of Naumburg where he read the proofs of the book and spent time with Lou Salomé, a prospective disciple. In the early fall of 1882, Nietzsche composed the *Hymn to Life* for mixed choir and orchestra based on the poem *Prayer to Life* by Salomé. He wrote in *Ecce Homo* that the "time will come when it will be sung in my memory."[17] It was published in October 1887.

1883-1885

Nietzsche wrote *Also Sprach Zarathustra: Ein Buch für Alle und Keinen* (*Thus Spoke Zarathustra: A Book for All and None*) during four short spurts of great creative energy over a two-year period from 1883 to 1885. "Except for these ten-day works, the years during and above all *after* my Zarathustra were marked by distress without equal. One pays dearly for immortality: one has to die several times while still alive."[18]

Nietzsche wrote the first part of *Zarathustra* in Rapallo in ten days at the end of January 1883. "*Zarathustra* came into being" during the cold and excessively rainy winter of 1882-1883 when Nietzsche stayed in Rapallo, which lies between Chiavari and Portofino, on the Gulf of Tigullio, less than thirty kilometers east of Genoa. In the morning, he would walk south on the road to Zoagli and in the afternoon, whenever his health permitted it, he walked through Santa Margherita Ligure to Portofino and back again. "It was on these two walks that the whole of *Zarathustra I* occurred to me, and especially Zarathustra himself as a type: rather, he *overtook me*."[19] After spending a few sick weeks in Genoa, Nietzsche moved to Rome for the spring. During one night in May on a *loggia* high above Piazza Barberini facing via delle Quattro Fontane, Nietzsche wrote the "Night Song" (in Z II), "the loneliest song [. . .] that has ever been written."[20]

Nietzsche wrote the second part of *Zarathustra* in Sils-Maria in two weeks at the end of June and the beginning of July 1883. "That summer, back home at the holy spot where the first lightning of the *Zarathustra* idea had flashed for me, I found *Zarathustra II*."[21] The "*Zarathustra* idea" is "the idea of the eternal recurrence." This idea

belongs in August 1881: it was penned on a sheet with the notation underneath, "6000 feet beyond man and time." That day I was walking through the woods along the lake of Silvaplana; at a powerful pyramidal rock not far from Surlei I stopped. It was then that this idea came to me.[22]

The Zarathustra stone – Nietzsche's "sacred stone"[23] – is on the northeastern shore of Lake Silvaplana.

Nietzsche wrote the third part of *Zarathustra* in Nice in two weeks at the beginning of January 1884. "The next winter, under the halcyon sky of Nizza [Nice], which then shone into my life for the first time, I found *Zarathustra III* – and was finished. Scarcely a year for the whole of it." The "decisive passage" entitled "On Old and New Tablets" in the third part was "composed on the most onerous ascent from the station to the marvelous Moorish eyrie, Eza."[24]

Nietzsche intended to end *Zarathustra* with the third part, but he wrote a fourth part in Nice in the winter of 1884-1885. The fourth and last part was intended to be the first of a second group of three parts, but Nietzsche later abandoned the idea.

The first (August 1883), second (January 1884), and third (April 1884) parts were published separately at first and then together in one volume in December 1886. The fourth and final part was printed privately in April 1885. All four parts were published together for the first time in March 1892, which was also the first public edition of the fourth and final part.

1885

Nietzsche began *Jenseits von Gut und Böse: Vorspiel einer Philosophie der Zukunft* (*Beyond Good and Evil: Prelude to a Philosophy of the Future*) in Sils-Maria in the summer of 1885 and completed it in Nice during the following winter. It was published in August 1886.

1886

For the "new edition" of *The Birth of Tragedy* published in October 1886, Nietzsche wrote a new introduction entitled "Versuch einer Selbstkritik" ("Attempt at a Self-Criticism"). He wrote this introduction in Sils-Maria in August 1886. The book also had a new title: *Die Geburt der Tragödie Oder: Griechenthum und Pessimismus* (*The Birth of Tragedy Or: Hellenism and Pessimism*).

A new edition of *Human, All Too Human* was published in October 1886 with the addition of *Assorted Opinions and Maxims* and *The Wanderer and his Shadow* as volume two. The original *Human, All Too Human* became volume one. Nietzsche wrote a new preface for each volume. The preface to Volume I was written in Nice in the spring of 1886, and the preface to Volume II was written in Sils-Maria in September 1886.

Nietzsche wrote the preface to the new edition of *Daybreak* in Ruta near Rapallo in the fall of 1886. It was published in June 1887.

1887

A new edition of *The Gay Science* was published in June 1887 with three substantial additions: a preface, Book V (sections 343-384), and an appendix of songs. Nietzsche also changed the title page, adding the subtitle *("la gaya scienza")* and replacing the quote from Ralph Waldo Emerson with one of his own. The new subtitle refers to "the Provençal concept of *gaya scienza* – that unity of *singer, knight,* and *free spirit* which distinguishes the wonderful early culture of the Provençals from all equivocal cultures."[25] The preface for the second edition was written in Ruta in the fall of 1886, Book V was written in Nice in November and December 1886, and the appendix of songs was "written for the most part in Sicily."[26] Nietzsche had visited Messina, Sicily, in April 1882 where he completed the first edition of *The Gay Science*.

Nietzsche wrote *Zur Genealogie der Moral: Eine Streitschrift* (*On the Genealogy of Morals: A Polemic*) as "A Sequel to My Last Book, *Beyond Good and Evil*, Which It Is Meant to Supplement and Clarify." He wrote the preface and first two essays in Sils-Maria during July 1887 and the third essay in September. The book was published in November 1887.

1888

Nietzsche began *Der Fall Wagner: Ein Musikanten-Problem* (*The Case of Wagner: A Musicians' Problem*) in Turin, Italy, in the spring of 1888 and completed it in Sils-Maria in July. It was published in September 1888.

In the summer of 1888, Nietzsche collected together for publication nine poems that he had composed from 1883 to 1888. He called the book *Dionysos-Dithyramben* (*Dithyrambs of Dionysus*). It was published with the complete *Thus Spoke Zarathustra* in 1892.

Nietzsche wrote *Götzen-Dämmerung oder Wie man mit dem Hammer philosophirt* (*Twilight of the Idols or How to Philosophize with a Hammer*) in Sils-Maria between the end of June and the beginning of September 1888, except for the foreword, which he wrote in Turin on 30 September 1888, the same day that he completed *The Anti-Christ*.[27] *Twilight of the Idols* was published in January 1889.

On the same day (3 September 1888) that Nietzsche finished *Twilight of the Idols* (except for the foreword), he began *Der Antichrist* (*The Anti-Christ*). It was originally subtitled *Umwertung aller Werte* (*Revaluation of All Values*), but he changed the subtitle to *Fluch auf das Christenthum* (*A Curse on Christianity*) just before his mental collapse at the beginning of 1889. Nietzsche wrote *The Anti-Christ* between 3 and 30 September 1888. The preface was written in Sils-Maria on 3 September 1888. He departed Sils-Maria on 20 September and on the next day arrived in Turin, where he moved into the same apartment that he had occupied in the spring, Via Carlo Alberto 6, fourth floor, opposite the Palazzo Carignano, with a view of the Piazza Carlo Alberto and of the hills beyond. Nietzsche completed the final quarter of *The Anti-Christ* here on 30 September.[28] It was published in 1895.

Nietzsche wrote his autobiographical book, *Ecce Homo: Wie man wird, was man ist* (*Ecce Homo: How One Becomes What One Is*) in Turin between 15 October 1888, his forty-fourth birthday, and 4 November. It was published in 1908.

Nietzsche wrote *Nietzsche contra Wagner: Aktenstücke eines Psychologen* (*Nietzsche contra Wagner: Out of the Files of a Psychologist*) in Turin in December 1888. It was published in 1895. Consisting of selected passages from his earlier books – "perhaps clarified here and there, above all, shortened," *Nietzsche contra Wagner* was intended to show that his break with Wagner occurred long before Nietzsche wrote *The Case of Wagner* in the summer of 1888. According to Nietzsche, the passages – "some go back all the way to 1877" – "leave no doubt" that he and Wagner are "antipodes."[29]

1889

On or about 3 January 1889, the forty-four-year-old Nietzsche collapsed in Turin's Piazza Carlo Alberto. Upon regaining consciousness, he was diagnosed as incurably insane. After little over a year in a psychiatric clinic in Jena, Nietzsche was released to the care of his mother at her house on Weingarten Street in Naumburg.

1894

In February 1894, Nietzsche's sister, Elisabeth, founded the Nietzsche Archives. Initially located at her mother's house on Weingarten Street, the Archives were moved to a larger house in the summer.

1895

In December 1895, Nietzsche's mother signed over her ownership of the Archives and Nietzsche's books to Elisabeth.

1896

In 1896, Elisabeth moved the Nietzsche Archives to Weimar.

1897

After the death of Nietzsche's mother in April 1897, Elisabeth obtained control of Nietzsche and then in July moved him into Villa Silberblick, the new home of his Archives in Weimar.

1900

Nietzsche died in Weimar on 25 August 1900, six weeks before his fifty-sixth birthday. Although he wanted to be buried on the Chastè peninsula of Lake Sils near Sils-Maria, Nietzsche was buried next to the church in Röcken alongside his father, mother, and infant brother.

1901

In 1901, Elisabeth published a selection from Nietzsche's notebooks of the years 1883 through 1888 that she entitled *Der Wille zur Macht: Versuch einer Umwertung aller Werte* (*The Will to Power: Attempt at a Revaluation of All Values*). A second expanded edition was published in 1906.

---

[1] EH I, §3.
[2] EH II, §1.
[3] EH II, §5.
[4] BT, Preface to Richard Wagner.
[5] EH-BT, §1.

[6] BT, Attempt at a Self-Criticism, §1.

[7] EH-BT, §1.

[8] BT, Attempt at a Self-Criticism, §1.

[9] Ibid.; EH-BT, §1.

[10] BT, Attempt at a Self-Criticism, §1.

[11] EH-HA, §1.

[12] EH-HA, §5.

[13] "By the summer of 1876, during the time of the first *Festspiele* [Bayreuth Festival], I said farewell to Wagner in my heart." NW, How I Broke Away from Wagner, §1.

[14] EH-HA, §5.

[15] EH I, §1.

[16] EH-GS.

[17] EH-Z, §1.

[18] EH-Z, §5.

[19] EH-Z, §1.

[20] EH-Z, §4.

[21] Ibid.

[22] EH-Z, §1.

[23] Sander L. Gilman, ed., *Conversations with Nietzsche: A Life in the Words of His Contemporaries*, trans. David J. Parent (Oxford: Oxford University Press, 1987), 161.

[24] EH-Z, §4.

[25] EH-GS.

[26] Ibid.

[27] EH-TI, §3.

[28] Ibid.

[29] NW, Preface.

FRIEDRICH NIETZSCHE

HERALD OF A NEW ERA

INTRODUCTION

Although Friedrich Nietzsche has been recognized as "one of the most original and influential figures in modern philosophy,"[1] there is still some confusion among us about the significance of his philosophy. The ideas of this late nineteenth-century German philosopher are important to us because Nietzsche is the herald of a new era that still, in many ways, has the potential to become reality.[2]

The death knell of the old era occurred when the belief in the Christian god had become unbelievable – a nineteenth-century European cultural event that Nietzsche summarized in the expression "God is dead." Caused by the "self-overcoming" of Christian belief by Christian morality, this event meant that the whole of Christian morality must now "collapse" because it was built upon this faith in a Christian god and that Christian morality must also "perish" as a result of its eventual self-overcoming by Christian truthfulness.

Even though he saw that "God is dead" and that Christian morality must eventually collapse and perish, Nietzsche condemned Christianity and wanted to "crush the infamy" because it corrupts humanity in two ways. As a slave morality, Christianity corrupts humanity by making it weaker. As an anti-natural morality, Christianity corrupts humanity by hindering the pursuit of knowledge and truth.

To become an anti-natural slave morality, Christianity (following the lead of Judaism) radically falsified the world and inverted the noble values of master morality (expressed in the dichotomy of good and bad) to create the *ressentiment* ("resentment") values of a slave morality (expressed in the dichotomy of good and evil). Master morality ("Roman," "pagan," "classical," "Renaissance") and slave morality (Judaism, Christianity) have been engaged in a struggle ever since the Jews

3

began this "slave revolt in morality" over two thousand years ago, a revolt that the Christians continued. Heretofore, the slave morality of Christianity and its heir, the democratic movement, have been victorious in this struggle.

In response to this victory of slave morality and to remedy Christianity's corruption of humanity, Nietzsche considered his life's task to be a "revaluation of all values," which means a new evaluation of all the *ressentiment* or slave values of Christian morality. Because slave values are the inversion of noble values, Nietzsche wanted to put things right side up again and create a new master morality in which the slave values of Christian morality are devalued and noble values are again at the top of the order of rank among values.

There are two aspects to Nietzsche's task: a personal and a public. The personal aspect is a "liberation" from all Christian moral values and has two parts: a "Yes-saying" part and a "No-saying, No-doing" part. The Yes-saying part of his task was accomplished in *Daybreak*, *The Gay Science*, and *Thus Spoke Zarathustra* and culminated in the "idea of the eternal recurrence." The No-saying, No-doing part was accomplished in *Beyond Good and Evil*, *On the Genealogy of Morals*, *Twilight of the Idols*, and *The Anti-Christ* and was intended to rekindle the struggle between master morality and slave morality and to ultimately lead to the victory of a new master morality.

Nietzsche called the public aspect of his task the "Great Noon." It is a moment of the "highest self-contemplation of humanity" at which the most elect, a new party of life, consecrate themselves to the "greatest of all tasks," "the higher breeding of humanity." The Great Noon inaugurates Nietzsche's new era in which a "philosophy of the future," his new master morality, replaces slave morality and a new nobility tackles the task of the higher breeding of humanity.

Nietzsche's idea of the eternal recurrence provides the basis of the philosophy of the future because "this highest formula of affirmation that is at all attainable" is the means for victory over slave morality. In addition to a new nobility and its task of the higher breeding of humanity, the essential elements of Nietzsche's philosophy of the future include concepts associated with his following expressions: "remain faithful to the earth," "will to power," "beyond good and evil," and "philosophers of the future."

Nietzsche intended his philosophy of the future, although incomplete, to serve as the intellectual foundation of a European cultural rebirth and the new nobility to serve as its institutional foundation. He called on philosophers of the future to complete the tasks of creating a new master morality and of establishing a new nobility.

The European cultural rebirth envisaged by Nietzsche also has a religious foundation. Not only does the idea of the eternal recurrence provide the basis of the philosophy of the future, it also provides the basis of the religion of the future. Nietzsche "baptized" this new "faith" with the name of a Greek god – Dionysus.

Chapter 1 explains the meaning of Nietzsche's expression that "God is dead." After Nietzsche's critique of Christianity both as a slave morality and as an anti-natural morality is provided in chapter 2, the next chapter analyzes Nietzsche's task of a revaluation of all values. Chapter 4 summarizes *Thus Spoke Zarathustra* and explains the concept of the Overman and the idea of the eternal recurrence. The next chapter sets forth the key concepts of Nietzsche's philosophy of the future and the following chapter demonstrates that Nietzsche's project of human enhancement is also a religious project. After chapter 7 elaborates on why Nietzsche thought he was a "destiny," the conclusion summarizes the proposal that Nietzsche is the herald of a new era.

---

[1] *The Encyclopedia of Philosophy*, s.v. "Nietzsche, Friedrich." In a more recent encyclopedia entry, the contributor wrote that "at the beginning of the twenty-first century, it would be difficult to find a philosopher whose influence on matters philosophical and cultural exceeds that of Nietzsche." *Encyclopedia of Philosophy*, 2nd ed., s.v. "Nietzsche, Friedrich."

[2] The argument could reasonably be made and has been made that many of Nietzsche's ideas did become manifest during the twentieth century. That historical inquiry, however, is beyond the scope of this work.

Chapter 1

GOD IS DEAD

The starting point for an understanding of Nietzsche's philosophy is a nineteenth-century European cultural event that he had witnessed during his lifetime. That event – "a generally European event"[1] and the "greatest recent event" – was that "God is dead," by which he meant "that the belief in the Christian god has become unbelievable."[2] In other words, "the faith in God has collapsed."[3] Nietzsche welcomed the death of the Christian god with cheerfulness and open arms because it permits the unhindered pursuit of knowledge and truth.

Although Nietzsche mentioned this lost faith in the Christian god in two of his early books,[4] he first proclaimed that "God is dead" in the first edition of *The Gay Science* (1882) in a section entitled "New struggles."

> After Buddha was dead, his shadow was still shown for centuries in a cave – a tremendous, gruesome shadow. God is dead; but given the way of men, there may still be caves for thousands of years in which his shadow will be shown. – And we – we still have to vanquish his shadow, too.[5]

In a latter section of the same book, Nietzsche elaborated on his proclamation that "God is dead" – and the implication that we have vanquished him – in the parable of "the madman." After entering a busy marketplace, the madman makes a speech, the gist of which is that "God is dead. God remains dead. And we have killed him."[6]

Expanding upon the meaning of the allegation that "we have killed God" in the second edition of *The Gay Science* (1887), Nietzsche explained that what "really triumphed over the Christian god" was "Christian morality itself, the concept of truthfulness that was understood ever more rigorously, the father confessor's refinement of the Christian conscience, translated and sublimated into a scientific conscience, into intellectual cleanliness at any price."[7] Through this "act of self-overcoming," Christianity "*as a dogma* was destroyed by its own morality." The resulting triumph of unconditionally honest atheism in the European conscience was "the awe-inspiring *catastrophe* of two thousand years of training in truthfulness that finally forbids itself the *lie involved in belief in God.*"[8] In other words, "the triumph of scientific atheism" and the "decline of the faith in the Christian god"[9] (i.e., the death of God) occurred simultaneously as the result of this "act of self-overcoming." That is how "we have killed God."

Written between the first and second editions of *The Gay Science*, the prologue of the first part of *Thus Spoke Zarathustra* (1883) contains Nietzsche's most famous statement that "God is dead." After ten years in the mountains enjoying his spirit and his solitude, Zarathustra descends the mountain to bring humanity a "gift"[10] – the "overman" (*der Übermensch*)[11] – and encounters an old saint who had not yet heard "that *God is dead!*"[12] Except for the old saint, Zarathustra mistakenly assumes that everybody else must know that God is dead. The lost faith in the Christian god provides the background for Zarathustra's speeches and actions during the remainder of the book. His initial intent is to teach the consequences of the death of God and to offer humanity a gift of a new meaning of the earth.[13] Zarathustra's speeches in the prologue, however, are ignored by the people.

Like Zarathustra's initial speeches, the madman's words that "we have killed God" fall on deaf ears. He realizes that he has come too early. He says to himself, "deeds, though done, still require time to be seen and heard. This deed is still more distant from them than the most distant stars – *and yet they have done it themselves.*"[14]

Nietzsche was one of the few nineteenth-century Europeans who saw that "God is dead" and who knew what this event really meant. Writing at the end of 1886, Nietzsche declared that this event "is already beginning to cast its first shadows over Europe." For all but a

7

few, however, this "event itself is far too great, too distant, too remote from the multitude's capacity for comprehension even for the tidings of it to be thought of as having *arrived* as yet. Much less may one suppose that many people know as yet *what* this event really means." To Nietzsche, this event meant that "much must collapse" – "for example, the whole of our European morality" – because it was "built upon this faith" in a Christian god. This impending collapse will involve a "long plenitude and sequence of breakdown, destruction, ruin, and cataclysm."[15]

In one of his last books, *Twilight of the Idols* (written in 1888), Nietzsche further explained this impending collapse of Christian morality.

> When one gives up Christian belief one thereby deprives oneself of the *right* to Christian morality. [. . .] Christianity is a system, a consistently thought out and *complete* view of things. If one breaks out of it a fundamental idea, the belief in God, one thereby breaks the whole thing to pieces: one has nothing of any consequence left in one's hands. Christianity presupposes that man does not know, *cannot* know what is good for him and what evil: he believes in God, who alone knows. Christian morality is a command: its origin is transcendental; it is beyond all criticism, all right to criticize; it possesses truth only if God is truth – it stands or falls with the belief in God.[16]

Not only will Christian morality "collapse" (*einfallen*) because of the death of the Christian god, but it will also "perish" (*zugrunde gehen*) because of the self-overcoming of Christian morality by Christian truthfulness. Just as Christian morality and its "will to truth" triumphed over the Christian god, "in the same way Christianity *as morality* must now perish, too: we stand on the threshold of *this* event." This event will happen when "Christian truthfulness" draws "its *most striking inference*, its inference *against* itself" and poses the question "*what is the meaning of all will to truth?*"[17]

> As the will to truth thus gains self-consciousness – there can be no doubt of that – morality will gradually *perish* now: this is the great spectacle in a hundred acts reserved for the

next two centuries in Europe – the most terrible, most questionable, and perhaps also the most hopeful of all spectacles. –[18]

Nietzsche welcomed the prospect of this "most hopeful of all spectacles" because knowledge and truth may then be pursued unhindered by Christian belief and morality. To Nietzsche and other "firstlings and premature births of the coming [twentieth] century," the consequences of the death of the Christian god were

> not at all sad and gloomy but rather like a new and scarcely describable kind of light, happiness, relief, exhilaration, encouragement, dawn.
>
> Indeed, we philosophers and "free spirits" feel, when we hear the news that "the old god is dead," as if a new dawn shone on us; our heart overflows with gratitude, amazement, premonitions, expectation. At long last the horizon appears free to us again, even if it should not be bright; at long last our ships may venture out again, venture out to face any danger; all the daring of the lover of knowledge is permitted again; the sea, *our* sea, lies open again; perhaps there has never yet been such an "open sea." –[19]

Before discussing what Nietzsche's metaphorical ships discovered on the "open sea" during this "new dawn," we must first examine his critique of Christianity. Even though he saw that "God is dead" and that consequently Christian morality must collapse and perish, Nietzsche condemned Christianity[20] and wanted to "*Ecrasez l'infâme!*" ("crush the infamy"), adopting Voltaire's motto in his eighteenth-century fight against the Christian church.[21] Or, as Zarathustra says, "O my brothers, am I cruel? But I say: what is falling, we should still push. Everything today falls and decays: who would check it? But I – I even want to push it."[22]

---

[1] GS, §357.
[2] GS, §343.
[3] GS, §358.
[4] HA I, §25; D, §96.

[5] GS, §108.
[6] GS, §125.
[7] GS, §357.
[8] GM III, §27.
[9] GS, §357.
[10] Z I, Prologue, §2.
[11] Z I, Prologue, §3.
[12] Z I, Prologue, §2.
[13] Laurence Lampert, *Nietzsche's Teaching: An Interpretation of "Thus Spoke Zarathustra"* (New Haven: Yale University Press, 1986), 17.
[14] GS, §125.
[15] GS, §343.
[16] TI IX, §5.
[17] GM III, §27.
[18] Ibid.
[19] GS, §343. Appropriately, Nietzsche entitled this section: "The meaning of our cheerfulness."
[20] A, §62. Just before his mental collapse at the beginning of 1889, Nietzsche changed the subtitle of *The Anti-Christ* from *Revaluation of All Values* to *A Curse on Christianity.* Julian Young, *Friedrich Nietzsche: A Philosophical Biography* (Cambridge: Cambridge University Press, 2010), 541.
[21] EH IV, §8.
[22] Z III, On Old and New Tablets, §20.

Chapter 2

CRITIQUE OF CHRISTIANITY

In his autobiographical book *Ecce Homo* (written in 1888),[1] Nietzsche defined himself by his relationship to Christianity. "What defines me, what sets me apart from the whole rest of humanity is that I *uncovered* Christian morality." He regarded the fact that humanity did not uncover Christian morality before he did "as the greatest uncleanliness that humanity has on its conscience [. . .] Blindness to Christianity is the crime *par excellence* – the crime against life."[2]

To express this act of uncovering of Christian morality in "a word that had the meaning of a provocation for everybody,"[3] Nietzsche called himself the "first immoralist."[4] He chose the word immoralist as "a symbol and badge of honor" for himself and was "proud" of having this word to distinguish him from "the whole of humanity."[5]

Nietzsche "uncovered" Christian morality by demonstrating how it corrupted humanity. He called Christian morality "the most malignant form of the will to lie, the real Circe of humanity – that which *corrupted* humanity."[6] Christianity is "the *corruptest* form of corruption."[7] In the climactic last section of *The Anti-Christ*, Nietzsche declared, "I *condemn* Christianity, I bring against the Christian Church the most terrible charge any prosecutor has ever uttered. To me it is the extremist thinkable form of corruption, it has had the will to the ultimate corruption conceivably possible."[8]

Nietzsche condemned Christianity because it corrupted and continues to corrupt humanity in two ways. First, Christianity corrupts humanity by making it weaker. It does so because Christian morality is a slave morality. Second, Christianity corrupts humanity by hindering the pursuit of knowledge and truth. It does so because Christian morality is an anti-natural morality.

A. Christianity as Slave Morality

Christian morality is a slave morality. As such, Christianity corrupts humanity by making it weaker through the inversion of the "good" of master morality into the "evil" of slave morality. In slave morality, consequently, the weak and powerless are the "good" and the strong and powerful are the "evil." This inversion is not only hostile to life, it negates life. Hostility to life and negation of life weaken humanity.

1. Inversion of Master Morality

Nietzsche asserted that Christianity was a product of *"ressentiment."* He used the French word for resentment because the German language lacked a word to adequately express the meaning he wanted to convey. His *ressentiment* theory of the origin of Christianity means "the birth of Christianity out of the spirit of *ressentiment,* not, as people may believe, out of the 'spirit' – a countermovement by its very nature, the great rebellion against the dominion of *noble* values."[9]

Noble values belong to what Nietzsche called noble morality, which is a morality characterized by the dichotomy of the concepts of good and bad. In noble morality, the origin of the concept and judgment "good" did not lie in what was "useful" or "practical"[10] nor in what was "unegoistic."[11] Rather, it lay in what was "noble" and "aristocratic."[12] The "good" originated in "the good" themselves,

> that is to say, the noble, powerful, high-stationed and high-minded, who felt and established themselves and their actions as good, that is, of the first rank, in contradistinction to all the low, low-minded, common and plebeian. It was out of this *pathos of distance* that they first seized the right to create values and to coin names for values: what had they to do with utility! [. . .] The pathos of nobility and distance, as aforesaid, the protracted and domineering fundamental total feeling on the part of a higher ruling order in relation to a lower order,

to a "below" – *that* is the origin of the antithesis "good" and "bad."[13]

The origin of the concept and judgment "bad," on the other hand, lay in what is "common," "plebeian," and "low."[14] In other words, the "opposition of 'good' and '*bad*' means approximately the same as 'noble' and 'contemptible.'"[15] "Good and bad is for a long time the same thing as noble and base, master and slave."[16]

To illustrate what he meant by noble morality, Nietzsche used the words "Roman," "pagan," "classical," and "Renaissance."[17] Reflecting his admiration of the Romans, he called them "the strong and noble, and nobody stronger and nobler has yet existed on earth or even been dreamed of."[18] As examples of "noble races," Nietzsche listed "the Roman, Arabian, Germanic, Japanese nobility, the Homeric heroes, the Scandinavian Vikings."[19] Referring to the Vikings, he wrote that the "Icelandic saga" is "almost" master morality's "most important document."[20]

Nietzsche also used the word "Aryan" (*der Arier*) to describe both a race[21] and its pre-Christian master morality as set forth in the "Law of Manu" from early Indian history.[22] This Aryan morality is "the means by which the *noble* orders, the philosophers and the warriors, keep the mob under control; noble values everywhere, a feeling of perfection, an affirmation of life, a triumphant feeling of well-being in oneself and of goodwill towards life – the *sun* shines on the entire book [i.e., the Law of Manu]."[23]

The antithetical concept to noble morality Nietzsche called "*ressentiment* morality."[24] He also called these two kinds of morality: "*master morality*" and "*slave morality*."[25] *Ressentiment* or slave morality "corresponds totally to Judeo-Christian morality." Nietzsche called it "Judeo-Christian morality" because Christianity "is *not* a counter-movement against the Jewish instinct, it is actually its logical consequence" and the Christian "is the *ultimate consequence of the Jews*."[26] After all, "the Jews are the inventors of Christianity."[27] Consequently, Christian morality is a *ressentiment* or slave morality because Jewish morality is a *ressentiment* or slave morality.

Ressentiment or slave morality was derived from a "*denial*" of noble or master morality.[28] This denial took the form of an inversion of noble

13

values. Through "an inversion of values," the Jews "mark the beginning of the slave rebellion in morals." "This inversion of values (which includes using the word 'poor' as synonymous with 'holy' and 'friend') constitutes the significance of the Jewish people."[29]

In opposing their enemies and conquerors, the Jews – that "priestly nation of *ressentiment par excellence*"[30] –

> were ultimately satisfied with nothing less than a radical re-valuation of their enemies' values, that is to say, an act of the *most spiritual revenge*. For this alone was appropriate to a priestly people, the people embodying the most deeply repressed priestly vengefulness. It was the Jews who, with awe-inspiring consistency, dared to invert the aristocratic value-equation (good = noble = powerful = beautiful = happy = beloved of God) and to hang on to this inversion with their teeth, the teeth of the most abysmal hatred (the hatred of impotence), saying "the wretched alone are the good; the poor, impotent, lowly alone are the good; the suffering, deprived, sick, ugly alone are pious, alone are blessed by God, blessedness is for them alone – and you, the powerful and noble, are on the contrary the evil, the cruel, the lustful, the insatiable, the godless to all eternity; and you shall be in all eternity the unblessed, accursed, and damned!"[31]

Nietzsche explained that the "slave revolt in morality begins when *ressentiment* itself becomes creative and gives birth to values." For example, the man of *ressentiment* conceived of the enemy as "the evil enemy" or "*the Evil One*," from which he evolved the concept of a "good one" – himself.[32] Thereby, the "good man" – "the noble, powerful man, the ruler" – of master morality became the "evil man" of slave morality.[33]

Christianity "inherited this Jewish revaluation"[34] of noble morality and, in its own "paradoxical formula 'god on the cross,' [. . .] promised a revaluation of all the values of antiquity."[35] In fulfilling this promise, Christianity became "the great rebellion against the dominion of *noble* values."[36]

Nietzsche described Christianity as the vengeful revolt of the Chandala, the name of the "untouchables" excluded from the Indian caste system. "Christianity is a revolt of everything that crawls along the ground directed against that which is *elevated*: the Gospel of the 'lowly' *makes* low."[37] Christianity is "a Chandala morality born of *ressentiment* and impotent revengefulness"[38] and "the slowly stirred-up fire of revengefulness, of Chandala revengefulness."[39]

> Christianity, growing from Jewish roots and comprehensible only as a product of this soil, represents the *reaction* against that [Aryan] morality of breeding, of race, of privilege – it is the *anti-Aryan* religion *par excellence*: Christianity the revaluation of all Aryan values, the victory of Chandala values, the evangel preached to the poor and lowly, the collective rebellion of everything downtrodden, wretched, ill-constituted, under-privileged against the "race" – undying Chandala revenge as the *religion of love* . . .[40]

As a result of this rebellion, the "greatest of all value-antitheses" today is between "*Christian* values" and "*noble* values";[41] "one cannot find a greater contrast than that between a *master morality* and the morality of *Christian* value concepts."[42] This great value-antithesis or contrast has manifested itself over the past two millennia in a "fearful struggle."[43]

Master morality and slave morality "have been engaged in a fearful struggle on earth for thousands of years."[44]

> The symbol of this struggle, inscribed in letters legible across all human history, is "Rome against Judea, Judea against Rome": – there has hitherto been no greater event than *this* struggle, *this* question, *this* deadly contradiction. Rome felt the Jew to be something like anti-nature itself, its antipodal monstrosity as it were: in Rome the Jew stood "*convicted* of hatred for the whole human race"; and rightly, provided one has a right to link the salvation and future of the human race with the unconditional dominance of aristocratic values, Roman values.[45]

15

Since the end of the Roman Empire, the age of the Renaissance has been "the last *great* age [. . .] when a higher order of values, the noble ones, those that say Yes to life, those that guarantee the future, had triumphed at the seat of the opposite values, those of *decline*."[46] The Renaissance was "an uncanny and glittering reawakening of the classical ideal, of the noble mode of evaluating all things."[47]

As "the last great cultural harvest," the Renaissance was the "*revaluation of Christian values*, the attempt, undertaken with every expedient, with every instinct, with genius of every kind, to bring about the victory of the opposing values, the *noble* values."[48] Europe, however, was robbed of this harvest by "this calamity of a monk"[49] named Martin Luther.

> This monk, all the vindictive instincts of a failed priest in him, fulminated in Rome *against* the Renaissance. [. . .] What Luther saw was the *corruption* of the Papacy, while precisely the opposite was palpably obvious: the old corruption, the *peccatum originale* ["original sin"], Christianity *no* longer sat on the Papal throne! Life sat there instead! the triumph of life! the great Yes to all lofty, beautiful, daring things! . . . And Luther *restored the Church*: he attacked it.[50]

As a consequence, "Judea immediately triumphed again, thanks to that thoroughly plebeian (German and English) *ressentiment* movement called the Reformation, and to that which was bound to arise from it, the restoration of the church – the restoration too of the ancient sepulchral repose of classical Rome."[51]

The "last great slave rebellion" began with the French Revolution.[52] With it, "Judea once again triumphed over the classical ideal" when "the last political noblesse in Europe, that of the *French* seventeenth and eighteenth century, collapsed beneath the popular instincts of *ressentiment*." In opposition to the French Revolution's "mendacious slogan of *ressentiment*, 'supreme rights of the majority,'" however, Napoleon appeared as "the *noble ideal as such* made flesh" with "the terrible and rapturous counterslogan 'supreme rights of the few'!"[53] "Napoleon, who considered modern ideas and civilization itself almost as a personal enemy, proved himself through this enmity as one of the greatest continuators of the Renaissance."[54]

Which of them has won *for the present*, Rome or Judea? But there can be no doubt: consider to whom one bows down in Rome itself today, as if they were the epitome of all the highest values – and not only in Rome but over almost half the earth, everywhere that man has become tame or desires to become tame: *three Jews*, as is known, and *one Jewess* (Jesus of Nazareth, the fisherman Peter, the rug weaver Paul, and the mother of the aforementioned Jesus, named Mary). This is very remarkable: Rome has been defeated beyond all doubt.[55]

The *"slave revolt in morality,"* which the Jews began over two thousand years ago and which the Christians continued, "has been victorious."[56] Because "a *nobler* disposition perished" by the victory of Christianity, Nietzsche declared that "Christianity has been up till now mankind's greatest misfortune."[57]

Moreover, the slave morality of Christianity – a *"herd animal morality"* – has expanded its domination through the democratic movement – a "visible expression" of herd animal morality – because "the *democratic* movement is the heir of the Christian movement."[58] The democratic movement transformed the Christian "falsehood" of the "equality of souls before God"[59] into the "poison of the doctrine '*equal* rights for all.'"[60]

To Nietzsche, "the democratic movement is not only a form of the decay of political organization but a form of the decay, namely the diminution, of man, making him mediocre and lowering his value."[61] In other words, the democratic movement, like Christianity, has weakened humanity.

2. Weakened Humanity

The result of the victory of the slave morality of Christianity and its heir, the democratic movement, is a weakened humanity because Christian morality's inversion of noble values is hostile to life and negates life. Both the hostility to life and the negation of life weaken humanity, which is thereby corrupted.

In Christianity, Nietzsche

> never failed to sense a *hostility to life* – a furious, vengeful antipathy to life itself. [. . .] Christianity was from the beginning, essentially and fundamentally, life's nausea and disgust with life, merely concealed behind, masked by, dressed up as, faith in "another" or "better" life. Hatred of "the world," condemnations of the passions, fear of beauty and sensuality, a beyond invented the better to slander this life, at bottom a craving for the nothing, for the end, for respite, for "the sabbath of sabbaths" – all this always struck me [. . .] as the most dangerous and uncanny form of all possible forms of a "will to decline" – at the very least a sign of abysmal sickness, weariness, discouragement, exhaustion, and the impoverishment of life.[62]

As "the religion of *pity*," Christianity is "*hostile to life*." Although "every *noble* morality" counts pity "as weakness," Christianity has "made of it *the* virtue, the ground and origin of all virtue." Yet, "life is denied, made *more worthy of denial* by pity." Pity "thwarts those instincts bent on preserving and enhancing the value of life."[63] In other words, pity weakens the ability to affirm life.

In addition, Christianity is "a conspiracy against health, beauty, well-constitutedness, bravery, intellect, *benevolence* of soul, *against life itself*."[64] In its campaign to exterminate the passions, Christianity attacked the passions at their roots, which "means to attack life at its roots: the practice of the Church is *hostile to life*."[65] Christian morality is "the actual poisoner and calumniator of life."[66]

Nietzsche called Christian morality "the revaluation of all values into hostility to life" and defined it as "the idiosyncrasy of decadents, with the ulterior motive of revenging oneself against life – successfully."[67] Explaining why nothing has preoccupied him more profoundly than the problem of decadence or decline, Nietzsche insisted, "Once one has developed a keen eye for the symptoms of decline, one understands [Christian] morality, too – one understands what is hiding under its most sacred names and value formulas: impoverished life, the will to the end, the great weariness. Morality negates life."[68]

Christian morality negates life instinctively. "God," "beyond," and "self-denial" are all "negations." Christian morality "impoverishes, pales and makes uglier the value of things, it *negates* the world. 'World' is a Christian term of abuse."[69] The Jews, however, "were the first to use the word 'world' as an opprobrium."[70] As "a will to negate life," Christian morality is "a secret instinct of annihilation, a principle of decay, diminution, and slander."[71] Christianity is the "denial of the will to life become religion!"[72]

As the "morality of decline *par excellence*," Christian morality is the "morality that would un-self man,"[73] by which Nietzsche meant that the Christian virtue of "selflessness" is actually the "loss of the center of gravity" and "resistance to the natural instincts,"[74] both of which are contrary to "the masterpiece of the art of self-preservation — of *selfishness*."[75] Christian morality, "that of un-selfing, reveals a will to the end; fundamentally, it negates life."[76] "If one shifts the center of gravity of life *out* of life into the 'Beyond' — into *nothingness* — one has deprived life as such of its center of gravity."[77]

Finally, the Christian conception of God is

> one of the most corrupt conceptions of God arrived at on earth [. . .] God degenerated to the *contradiction of life*, instead of being its transfiguration and eternal *Yes*! In God a declaration of hostility towards life, nature, the will to life! God the formula for every calumny of "this world," for every lie about "the next world"! In God nothingness deified, the will to nothingness sanctified! . . . [78]

By its hostility to life and negation of life, Christianity weakened humanity. Humanity is weakened when life is denied, devalued, impoverished, and no longer its own center of gravity. Such a weakened and sick humanity is a corrupt humanity.

Using the pagan Germans as an historical example, Nietzsche declared that Christianity was "*poison*" to "youthful, vigorous barbarians" because "to implant the teaching of sinfulness and damnation into the heroic, childish and animal soul of the ancient German, for example, is nothing other than to poison it" and "thus in the longer run a fundamental enfeeblement of such barbarians."[79] Rather than "improving" humanity as the Christian church maintained, Christianity actually weakened and thus corrupted humanity through "the *taming* of the beast man."[80]

> In the early Middle Ages, when the Church was in fact above all a menagerie, one everywhere hunted down the fairest specimens of the "blond beast" – one "improved," for example, the noble Teutons. But what did such a Teuton afterwards look like when he had been "improved" and led into a monastery? Like a caricature of a human being, like an abortion: he had become a "sinner," he was in a cage, one had imprisoned him behind nothing but sheer terrifying concepts. . . . There he lay now, sick, miserable, filled with ill-will towards himself; full of hatred for the impulses towards life, full of suspicion of all that was still strong and happy. In short, a "Christian." . . . In physiological terms: in the struggle with the beast, making it sick *can* be the only means of making it weak. This the Church understood: it *corrupted* the human being, it weakened him – but it claimed to have "improved" him . . .[81]

"Improved" signified to Nietzsche "the same thing as 'tamed,' 'weakened,' 'discouraged,' 'made refined,' 'made effete,' 'emasculated' (thus almost the same thing as *harmed*)."[82] Christianity used "the holy pretext of 'improving' mankind, as the ruse for sucking the blood of life itself. Morality as vampirism."[83]

Furthermore, "Christianity desires to dominate *beasts of prey*; its means for doing so is to make them *sick* – weakening is the Christian recipe for taming, for 'civilization.'"[84] "Christianity *needs* sickness [. . .] – *making* sick is the true hidden objective of the Church's whole system of salvation procedures."[85] Thus, "sickness belongs to the essence of Christianity."[86]

As "a single will" dominating Europe for eighteen centuries, Christianity has turned "man into a *sublime miscarriage*." Today's European represents the "almost deliberate degeneration and atrophy of man." The "spiritual men" of Christianity "have so far held sway over the fate of Europe, with their 'equal before God,' until finally a smaller, almost ridiculous type, a herd animal, something eager to please, sickly, and mediocre has been bred, the European of today —"[87]

B. Christianity as Anti-natural Morality

Christian morality is an anti-natural morality.[88] The corollary of Christianity as a slave morality is Christianity as an anti-natural morality because a slave morality is an inversion of master morality. Since a master morality is an expression of natural values, an inversion of master morality results in anti-natural values. Therefore, the values of a slave morality are anti-natural.

In conjunction with the inversion of master morality, Christianity became an anti-natural morality by radically falsifying the world. This radical falsification of the world resulted in a morality that is hostile to reality and all that is natural, including natural values. Christian morality's hostility to reality and lack of nature corrupts humanity by hindering the pursuit of knowledge and truth.

1. Radical Falsification of the World

Just as the Jews were the first to invert the noble values of master morality, they were also the first to radically falsify the world.

The Jews are the most remarkable nation of world history because, faced with the question of being or not being, they preferred, with a perfectly uncanny conviction, being *at any price*: the price they had to pay was the radical *falsification* of all nature, all naturalness, all reality, the entire inner world as well as the outer. They defined themselves *counter* to all those conditions under which a nation was previously able to live, was *permitted* to live; they made of themselves an antithesis to *natural* conditions – they inverted religion, religious worship, morality, history, psychology one after the other in an irreparable way into the *contradiction of their natural values*. We encounter the same phenomenon again [in Christianity] and in unutterably vaster proportions, although only as a copy – the Christian Church, in contrast to the "nation of saints," renounces all claim to originality.[89]

Because it is the "logical consequence" of the "Jewish instinct,"[90] Christianity inherited this Jewish falsification of the world. Christianity also inherited the Jewish "history of the *denaturalizing* of natural values"[91] because the radical falsification of the world required the denaturalization of nature and the devaluation of natural values.

On this Jewish-falsified soil arose Christianity, "a form of mortal hostility to reality as yet unsurpassed." Christianity "negated the last remaining form of reality, the 'holy people,' the 'chosen people,' the *Jewish* reality itself." The "little rebellious movement which is baptized with the name of Jesus of Nazareth" was a "revolt against the Jewish Church [. . .] against 'the good and the just,' against 'the saints of Israel,' against the social hierarchy [. . .] against caste, privilege, the order, the social form; it was *disbelief* in 'higher men,' a *No* uttered towards everything that was priest and theologian," but it was

> the Jewish instinct *once more* – in other words the priestly instinct which can no longer endure the priest as a reality, the invention of an even *more abstract* form of existence, an even *more unreal* vision of the world than one conditioned by an organized Church. Christianity *negates* the [Jewish] Church . . .[92]

Furthermore, because the "only driving element in the roots of Christianity" is an "instinctive hatred *for* actuality," the "Christian's world of ideas contains nothing which so much as touches upon actuality."[93]

> In Christianity neither morality nor religion come into contact with reality at any point. Nothing but imaginary *causes* ("God," "soul," "ego," "spirit," "free will" – or "unfree will"): nothing but imaginary *effects* ("sin," "redemption," "grace," "punishment," "forgiveness of sins"). A traffic between imaginary *beings* ("God," "spirits," "souls"); an imaginary *natural* science (anthropocentric; complete lack of the concept of natural causes); an imaginary *psychology* (nothing

but self-misunderstandings, interpretations of pleasant or un-pleasant general feelings, for example the condition of the *nervus sympathicus* ["sympathetic nerves"], with the aid of the sign-language of religio-moral idiosyncrasy – "repentance," "sting of conscience," "temptation by the Devil," "the prox-imity of God"); an imaginary *teleology* ("the kingdom of God," "the Last Judgment," "eternal life"). – This purely fictitious world is distinguished from the world of dreams, very much to its disadvantage, by the fact that the latter *mirrors* actuality, while the former falsifies, disvalues and denies actuality. Once the concept "nature" had been devised as the concept antithetical to "God," "natural" had to be the word for "rep-rehensible" – this entire fictional world has its roots in *hatred* of the natural (- actuality! -), it is the expression of a profound discontent with the actual.[94]

What horrified Nietzsche about Christian morality was its "lack of na-ture" and "the utterly gruesome fact that *antinature* itself received the highest honors as morality and was fixed over humanity as law and categorical imperative."[95]

As a consequence of this hostility to reality and lack of nature, Christianity's anti-natural morality is full of lies. "*All* the concepts of the Church are [. . .] the most malicious false-coinage there is for the purpose of *disvaluing* nature and natural values."[96] As the thinker who uncovered Christian morality, Nietzsche also uncovered "the disvalue of all [Christian] values that are and have been believed."[97]

What Christianity called "truth," Nietzsche recognized as "the most harmful, insidious, and subterranean form of lie."[98] He defined a lie as "wanting *not* to see something one does see, wanting not to see something *as* one sees it."[99] He also defined a lie as "not *wanting* to see at any price how reality is constituted fundamentally."[100]

Standing "in opposition to the mendaciousness of millennia," Nietzsche called himself "the first *decent* human being" because he was "the first to *discover* the truth by being the first to experience lies as lies – smelling them out. – My genius is in my nostrils."[101] In this way, Nietzsche's "lightning bolt of truth"[102] uncovered Christian morality.

The "truth" speaks out of him, but his "truth is *terrible*; for so far one has called *lies* truth."[103]

Although not morally opposed to the lie as such, Nietzsche was opposed to the lie as a means when the ends are bad.

> – Ultimately the point is to what *end* a lie is told. That "holy" ends are lacking in Christianity is *my* objection to its means. Only *bad* ends: the poisoning, slandering, denying of life, contempt for the body, the denigration and self-violation of man through the concept sin – *consequently* its means too are bad.[104]

In addition to "lie," another term that Nietzsche used to describe what Christianity called "truth" was "idols," as used in the title of his book *Twilight of the Idols*. "What is called *idol* on the title page is simply what has been called truth so far."[105]

Nietzsche also used the words "ideals" and "idealism" in the same sense as idols. Idols is "my word for 'ideals.'"[106] In *Human, All Too Human*, Nietzsche claimed that he liberated himself from what in his nature did not belong to him, for example, "idealism." The "title means: 'where *you* see ideal things, *I* see what is – human, alas, all-too-human!' – I know man better."[107] By "idealism," Nietzsche meant the "innermost *cowardice* before reality, which is also cowardice before the truth," and "untruthfulness which has become instinctive."[108]

> The *lie* of the ideal has so far been the curse on reality; on account of it, mankind itself has become mendacious and false down to its most fundamental instincts – to the point of worshipping the *opposite* values of those which alone would guarantee its health, its future, the lofty *right* to its future.[109]

Defining "error" as "faith in the ideal," Nietzsche said error was "not blindness" but "*cowardice*." "Every attainment, every step forward in knowledge, *follows* from courage, from hardness against oneself, from cleanliness in relation to oneself."[110] He equated knowledge with "saying Yes to reality," which requires courage and an excess of strength. Just as knowledge is necessary for the strong, the "ideal" – "cowardice and the flight from reality" – is necessary "for the weak, who are inspired by weakness." The weak "are not free to know: the decadents *need* the lie."[111] As decadents, Christians need the lie. They are not free to know.

2. Hindrance to the Pursuit of Knowledge and Truth

As a result of Christianity's anti-natural morality, humanity is corrupted because the pursuit of knowledge and truth through science is hindered. Not only does Christianity value revelation higher than science as the source of truth, Christianity also hinders science through its concept of sin and other lies.[112]

For the Christian, high above all of the sciences are the "revealed truth" and the "eternal salvation of the soul." Therefore, the "truly Christian judgment about science" is that it is "something second-class, not anything ultimate, unconditional, not an object of passion."[113] In addition to its low opinion of science, Christianity is hostile to science.

Because, as just discussed,[114] Christianity "is at no point in contact with actuality," it "must naturally be a mortal enemy of the 'wisdom of the world,' that is to say of *science*. [. . .] 'Faith' as an imperative is a *veto* against science – *in praxis* ["in practice"] the lie at any cost."[115] "'Faith' means not *wanting* to know what is true."[116]

The "natural concept 'cause' and 'effect'" is once and for all stood on its head" by "that most mendacious mode of interpretation of a supposed 'moral world-order'" when "priestly agitators [. . .] interpret all good fortune as a reward, all misfortune as punishment for disobedience of God, for 'sin.'" "When one has banished natural causality from the world by means of reward and punishment, one then requires an *anti-natural* causality: all the remaining unnaturalness follows forthwith."[117]

As "the sound conception of cause and effect," science is the "*one great danger*" the priest knows to his rule. Consequently, the "concept of guilt and punishment, the entire 'moral world-order,' was invented *in opposition to* science – *in opposition to* the detaching of man from the priest." Furthermore, the "concept of guilt and punishment, including the doctrine of 'grace,' of 'redemption,' of 'forgiveness' – *lies* through and through and without any psychological reality – were invented to

25

destroy the *causal sense* of man: they are an outrage on the concept cause and effect!"[118]

> When the natural consequences of an act are no longer "natural" but thought of as effected by the conceptual ghosts of superstition, by "God," by "spirits," by "souls," as merely "moral" consequences, as reward, punishment, sign, chastisement, then the precondition for knowledge has been destroyed – *then one has committed the greatest crime against humanity.* – Sin, to say it again, that form *par excellence* of the self-violation of man, was invented to make science, culture, every kind of elevation and nobility of man impossible; the priest *rules* through the invention of sin. –[119]

Moreover, sin is a Jewish invention. "Sin, as it is now experienced wherever Christianity holds sway or has held sway, is a Jewish feeling and a Jewish invention. Regarding this background of all Christian morality, Christianity did aim to 'Judaize' the world."[120] Here, as earlier, Nietzsche's critique of Christianity is also a critique of Judaism.

Nietzsche uncovered "Judeo-Christian morality"[121] by showing how it corrupted and continues to corrupt humanity through its inversion of master morality and radical falsification of the world. Hitherto, this anti-natural slave morality – Judeo-Christian morality – and its heir, the democratic movement, have been victorious in the centuries-long struggle between Rome and Judea.

---

[1] *Ecce Homo* means "Behold the man." These were the words that Pontius Pilate, the Roman governor of Judea, allegedly uttered in presenting Jesus to his orthodox Jewish accusers. John 19:5.
[2] EH IV, §7.
[3] Ibid.
[4] EH IV, §2.
[5] EH IV, §6.
[6] EH IV, §7. Circe was the Greek goddess of magic who transformed Odysseus' men into swine. Homer *Odyssey* 10.211-60.
[7] A, §58.
[8] A, §62.
[9] EH-GM.
[10] GM I, §3.
[11] GM I, §2.

[12] GM I, §4.
[13] GM I, §2.
[14] GM I, §4.
[15] BGE, §260.
[16] HA I, §45.
[17] CW, Epilogue.
[18] GM I, §16.
[19] GM I, §11. At the bottom of all these noble races, Nietzsche saw "the beast of prey, the splendid *blond beast* prowling about avidly in search of spoil and victory." Ibid.
[20] CW, Epilogue.
[21] Nietzsche called the Aryan "the conqueror and *master race.*" GM I, §5.
[22] TI VII, §§3-4.
[23] A, §56.
[24] A, §24.
[25] BGE, §260. To clarify that these two kinds of morality are not mutually exclusive, Nietzsche immediately added "that in all the higher and more mixed cultures there also appear attempts at mediation between these two moralities, and yet more often the interpenetration and mutual misunderstanding of both, and at times they occur directly alongside each other – even in the same human being, within a *single* soul." Ibid.
[26] A, §24.
[27] GS, §99.
[28] A, §24.
[29] BGE, §195.
[30] GM I, §16.
[31] GM I, §7.
[32] GM I, §10.
[33] GM I, §11.
[34] GM I, §7.
[35] BGE, §46.
[36] EH-GM.
[37] A, §43.
[38] A, §45.
[39] A, §58. "As a European movement, the Christian movement has been from the very first a collective movement of outcast and refuse elements of every kind [. . .] Christianity has at its basis the *rancune* ["grudge" or "rancor"] of the sick, the instinct directed *against* the healthy, *against* health. Everything well-constituted, proud, high-spirited, beauty above all, is hurtful to its ears and eyes." A, §51.
[40] TI VII, §4.
[41] A, §37.
[42] CW, Epilogue.
[43] GM I, §16.
[44] Ibid.
[45] Ibid.

[46] EH-CW, §2.
[47] GM I, §16.
[48] A, §61.
[49] EH-CW, §2.
[50] A, §61.
[51] GM I, §16.
[52] BGE, §46. The French Revolution "aimed at the 'brotherhood' of nations and a blooming universal exchange of hearts." GS, §362.
[53] GM I, §16.
[54] GS, §362.
[55] GM I, §16.
[56] GM I, §7.
[57] A, §51.
[58] BGE, §202.
[59] A, §62.
[60] A, §43.
[61] BGE, §203.
[62] BT, Attempt at a Self-Criticism, §5.
[63] A, §7.
[64] A, §62.
[65] TI V, §1.
[66] TI VI, §6.
[67] EH IV, §7.
[68] CW, Preface.
[69] CW, Epilogue.
[70] BGE, §195.
[71] BT, Attempt at a Self-Criticism, §5.
[72] EH-CW, §2.
[73] EH IV, §7.
[74] EH-D, §2.
[75] EH II, §9.
[76] EH IV, §7.
[77] A, §43.
[78] A, §18.
[79] HA II1, §224.
[80] TI VII, §2.
[81] Ibid.
[82] GM III, §21.
[83] EH IV, §8.
[84] A, §22.
[85] A, §51.
[86] A, §52.
[87] BGE, §62. "The *sick* are man's greatest danger; *not* the evil, *not* the 'beasts of prey.' Those who are failures from the start, downtrodden, crushed – it is they, the *weakest*, who must undermine life among men, who call into question and poison

most dangerously our trust in life, in man, and in ourselves." GM III, §14.

[88] "All naturalism in morality, that is all *healthy* morality, is dominated by an instinct of life [. . .] *Anti-natural* morality, that is virtually every morality that has hitherto been taught, reverenced and preached, turns on the contrary precisely *against* the instincts of life." TI V, §4.

[89] A, §24. Nietzsche also called the Jews "the most *fateful* nation in world history" because "their after-effect has falsified mankind to such an extent that today the Christian is able to feel anti-Jewish without realizing he is the *ultimate consequence of the Jews*." Ibid. Nietzsche's idea that "the Christian is only a Jew of a *'freer'* confession," A, §44, explains his negative opinion of Christian anti-Semitism. Nietzsche considered the Jews as a race. See passage quoted at n. 191 on p. 88 below.

[90] A, §24.

[91] A, §25.

[92] A, §27.

[93] A, §39.

[94] A, §15.

[95] EH IV, §7.

[96] A, §38. "In Christianity, as the art of holy lying, the whole of Judaism, a schooling and technique pursued with the utmost seriousness for hundreds of years, attains its ultimate perfection. The Christian, that *ultima ratio* ["final argument"] of the lie, is the Jew once more – even *thrice* more." A, §44.

[97] EH IV, §8.

[98] Ibid.

[99] A, §55.

[100] EH IV, §4.

[101] EH IV, §1. Nietzsche despised the "man of today" because everyone knows that "there is no longer any 'God,' any 'sinner,' any 'redeemer,' – that 'free will,' 'moral world-order' are lies." Yet, "*everyone nonetheless remains unchanged.* [. . .] what a *monster of falsity* modern man must be that he is nonetheless *not ashamed* to be called a Christian!" A, §38.

[102] EH IV, §8.

[103] EH IV, §1.

[104] A, §56.

[105] EH-TI, §1.

[106] EH, Preface, §2.

[107] EH-HA, §1.

[108] EH-CW, §2.

[109] EH, Preface, §2.

[110] EH, Preface, §3.

[111] EH-BT, §2.

[112] Although not true for the majority of traditional Christians, Nietzsche never felt hindered by the concept of sin in his own pursuit of knowledge despite his religious upbringing as a Lutheran pastor's son. In *Ecce Homo*, he revealed that it had "escaped me altogether in what way I was supposed to be 'sinful.' Likewise, I lack

any reliable criterion for recognizing the bite of conscience." EH II, §1.

[113] GS, §123.

[114] See chap. 2, sect. B, subsect. 1, above.

[115] A, §47.

[116] A, §52.

[117] A, §25.

[118] A, §49.

[119] Ibid.

[120] GS, §135.

[121] A, §24.

Chapter 3

REVALUATION OF ALL VALUES

In response to the victory of slave morality and to remedy Christianity's corruption of humanity, Nietzsche considered his life's "task" to be "a *revaluation of all values.*"[1] His task was not only a "liberation" from all Christian moral values,[2] it was also an act of "the highest self-contemplation of humanity."[3] The former may be regarded as the personal aspect of Nietzsche's task, and the latter may be regarded as the public aspect. Combining these two aspects, Nietzsche declared that the revaluation of all values (*die Umwertung aller Werte*) is "my formula for an act of the highest self-contemplation of humanity, become flesh and genius in me."[4]

In answering the question in *Ecce Homo, "how one becomes what one is,*"[5] Nietzsche revealed that his life's "task" was "a *revaluation of all values.*" He was not always conscious of this task because to "become what one is, one must not have the faintest notion *what* one is."[6] Nietzsche expressed this retrospective view of his life's task in his writings of 1888 in which he claimed that his task was unconsciously manifested in two of his earlier writings.[7]

With *Daybreak* (1881), Nietzsche could finally state that his self-conscious "campaign against [Christian] morality begins."[8] It was when he "first took up the fight against the morality that would unself man."[9] Here, he "commenced to undermine our *faith in morality*"[10] and claimed that "in this book faith in morality is withdrawn."[11]

Daybreak opens with the Indian inscription: "There are so many dawns that have not yet glowed." Nietzsche sought that new morning in "a *revaluation of all values,* in a liberation from all moral values, in saying Yes to and having confidence in all that has hitherto been forbidden, despised, and damned." At the same time, *Daybreak* "contains no negative word, no attack, no spite." "Morality is not attacked, it is merely no longer in the picture." For that reason, Nietzsche called it a "Yes-saying book."[12]

Nietzsche divided the personal aspect of his task between the Yes-saying part and the No-saying, No-doing part. Just as *Daybreak* is a "Yes-saying book," the "same is true also and in the highest degree"[13] of his next book, *The Gay Science*. With the completion of *Thus Spoke Zarathustra* in 1885, he announced that "the Yes-saying part of my task had been solved."[14] We shall see in the next chapter how Nietzsche solved the Yes-saying part of his task.

In the section in *Ecce Homo* on *Daybreak*, Nietzsche explained that his task of a revaluation of all values

> follows of necessity from the insight that humanity is *not* all by itself on the right way, that it is by no means governed divinely, that, on the contrary, it has been precisely among its holiest value concepts that the instinct of denial, corruption, and decadence has ruled seductively. [. . .] The demand that we should believe that everything is really in the best of hands, that a book, the Bible, offers us definitive assurances about the divine governance and wisdom in the destiny of man, is – translated back into reality – the will to suppress the truth about the pitiable opposite of all this; namely, that humanity has so far been in the *worst* of hands and that it has been governed by the underprivileged, the craftily vengeful, the so-called "saints," these slanderers of the world and violators of man.[15]

Nietzsche's "insight" here later developed into his uncovering of Christianity's true origins as a product of *ressentiment* and of Christian morality's true character as an anti-natural slave morality. This uncovering, primarily accomplished in *Beyond Good and Evil* (1886), *On the Genealogy of Morals* (1887), *Twilight of the Idols* (written in 1888), and *The Anti-Christ* (written in 1888), constitutes the No-saying, No-doing part of the personal aspect of his task. Nevertheless, Nietzsche saw no contradiction between the two parts of this aspect of his task because he "does not know how to separate doing No from saying Yes"[16] and because "negating *and destroying* are conditions of saying Yes."[17] In other words, in order to create, something must first be destroyed.

Beyond Good and Evil began "the No-saying, *No-doing* part: the revaluation of our values so far, the great war – conjuring up a day of decision. This included the slow search for those related to me, those who, prompted by strength, would offer me their hands for *destroying*."[18] Nietzsche's intent with this book was to rekindle "that greatest of all conflicts of ideals [between Rome and Judea]," namely, the "great war" between master morality and slave morality. That was "the aim of that dangerous slogan" – beyond good and evil – inscribed at the head of the book.[19]

Calling himself a "psychologist" as he often did, Nietzsche revealed in *Ecce Homo* that *On the Genealogy of Morals* contains three "decisive preliminary studies by a psychologist for a revaluation of all values."[20] The most important of these studies is the first inquiry in which he introduced his *ressentiment* theory of the origin of Christian morality. He considered the "question concerning the origin of [Christian] moral values [. . .] a question of the very first rank because it is crucial for the future of humanity."[21] The study of the origin of Christian moral values is crucial for the future of humanity because an effective critique and revaluation of these values require knowledge of their origin.

Nietzsche asserted that "we need a *critique* of [Christian] moral values, *the value of these values themselves must first be called in question* – and for that there is needed a knowledge of the conditions and circumstances in which they grew, under which they evolved and changed [. . .], a knowledge of a kind that has never yet existed or even been desired."[22] He provided this knowledge in his "genealogy" or natural history of morals, the gist of which was discussed in his critique of Christianity in the last chapter.

In *Twilight of the Idols*, Nietzsche offered "a quick idea how before me everything stood on its head,"[23] that is, how Christian morality was an inversion of master morality. Nietzsche's revaluation of all values was his attempt to put things right-side up again: "nobody before me knew the right way, the way *up*; it is only beginning with me that there are hopes again, tasks, ways that can be prescribed for culture – *I am he that brings these glad tidings.*"[24] Besides glad tidings, the revaluation of all values may also bring foreboding. He called a revaluation of all values "this questionmark so black, so huge it casts a shadow over him who sets it up – such a destiny of a task compels one every instant to run out into the sunshine so as to shake off a seriousness grown all too oppressive."[25]

As already mentioned,[26] "idols" was one of the terms Nietzsche used to describe what Christianity called "truth." The title *Twilight of the Idols* meant that "the old truth is approaching its end."[27] In this book, Nietzsche accelerated the approach of this end by the "sounding-out of idols." The *"eternal* idols" of Christianity are "here touched with the hammer as with a tuning fork – there are no more ancient idols in existence. . . . Also none more hollow." That is the meaning of the book's subtitle, *How to Philosophize with a Hammer.* That is also the reason Nietzsche called this "little book [. . .] a *grand declaration of war.*"[28]

Later in the same book, Nietzsche provided his first example of his revaluation of all values.

> The most general formula at the basis of every religion and morality is: "Do this and this, refrain from this and this – and you will be happy! Otherwise . . ." Every morality, every religion *is* this imperative – I call it the great original sin of reason, *immortal unreason.* In my mouth this formula is converted into its reverse – *first* example of my "revaluation of all values": a well-constituted human being, a "happy one," *must* perform certain actions and instinctively shrinks from other actions, he transports the order of which he is the physiological representative into his relations with other human beings and with things. In a formula: his virtue is the *consequence* of his happiness.[29]

On the same day that Nietzsche finished *Twilight of the Idols,* he began *The Anti-Christ,* the first of four parts of his planned book to be entitled *Revaluation of All Values.*[30] In *The Anti-Christ,* Nietzsche declared that "*we ourselves,* we free spirits, are already a 'revaluation of all values,' an *incarnate* declaration of war and victory over all ancient conceptions of 'true' and 'untrue.'"[31] In the last section of the book, he

34

condemned Christianity and rhetorically asked why not calculate time from the last day of Christianity – from the day he completed *The Anti-Christ* – and then ended the section and thus the book with the words: "Revaluation of all values!"[32]

Despite *The Anti-Christ* being the only completed book of his planned *magnum opus*,[33] Nietzsche had the highest hope for its historical impact. He "attacked the tremendous task" of writing *The Anti-Christ* "with a sovereign feeling of pride that was incomparable, certain at every moment of my immortality, engraving sign upon sign on bronze tablets with the sureness of a destiny."[34] *The Anti-Christ* is "the shattering lightning bolt [. . .] that will make the earth convulse."[35]

Referring to *The Anti-Christ*, which had already been written, Nietzsche explained in the first sentence of *Ecce Homo* that he wrote this autobiographical book in order to say who he was because he would soon "confront humanity with the most difficult demand ever made of it." He intended *Ecce Homo* to be published before *The Anti-Christ* in order to explain *"who I am"* so people *"do not mistake me for someone else."*[36] The "most difficult demand" is the revaluation of all values in the sense of a public act that Nietzsche called upon humanity to perform.

Having accomplished the personal aspect of his task in his earlier books, Nietzsche now challenged humanity in his last books to perform the public aspect of his task. In other words, he accomplished the personal aspect of his task with his uncovering of Christian morality. With that accomplishment, he had completed preparations for "a moment of the highest self-contemplation of humanity."[37] He called this moment "a *great noon* when it looks back and far forward, when it emerges from the dominion of accidents and priests and for the first time poses, *as a whole*, the question of Why? and For What?"[38]

The Great Noon (*der grosse Mittag*) is that event "at which the most elect consecrate themselves for the greatest of all tasks." The "most elect" are also called that "new party of life which would tackle the greatest of all tasks, the higher breeding of humanity."[39] If the "greatest of all tasks" is "the higher breeding of humanity," then the "great noon" is that event at which the most elect or new party of life answers the questions of Why? and For What? by consecrating itself to the task of the higher breeding of humanity. In other words, the Great Noon is that event when the most elect or new party of life contemplates the

35

purpose and goal of its existence (the questions of Why? and For What?), finds that purpose to be the higher breeding of humanity and the goal, as we shall see,[40] to be the enhancement of humanity, and declares that purpose and goal to be sacred. Nietzsche anticipated this event with his *Thus Spoke Zarathustra*. That is the meaning of his description of the "*event of Zarathustra*" as "the act of a tremendous purification and consecration of humanity."[41]

---

[1] EH II, §9. The "revaluation of all values" can be thought of as Nietzsche's term for a "moral revolution." Young, *Nietzsche*, 407.

[2] EH-D, §1.

[3] EH-D, §2. Kaufmann's translation has been modified. He translated "höchster Selbstbesinnung der Menschheit" in two different ways: as "highest self-examination for humanity," ibid., and as "supreme self-examination on the part of humanity." EH IV, §1. The word "self-contemplation" is used here and elsewhere in this book instead because it is a more accurate translation of *Selbstbesinnung* than "self-examination." *Langenscheidt Collins Grosswörterbuch Englisch*, 6th ed., s.v. "Selbstbesinnung."

[4] EH IV, §1. Kaufmann's translation has been modified. See previous note.

[5] *Ecce Homo* is subtitled *How One Becomes What One Is*.

[6] EH II, §9.

[7] TI X, §5 (referring to *The Birth of Tragedy*); EH-HA, §6 (referring to *Human, All Too Human*).

[8] EH-D, §1. *Daybreak* is subtitled *Thoughts on the Prejudices of Morality*.

[9] EH-D, §2.

[10] D, Preface, §2.

[11] D, Preface, §4. In discussing Christian morality, Nietzsche often dropped the "Christian" modifier, but it is clear from the context that what Nietzsche meant here and in the three previous quotations, as well as in many other places, is *Christian* morality and not morality in general.

[12] EH-D, §1.

[13] EH-GS.

[14] EH-BGE, §1.

[15] EH-D, §2.

[16] EH IV, §2.

[17] EH IV, §4.

[18] EH-BGE, §1. "From this moment forward all my writings are fish hooks [. . .] If nothing was caught, I am not to blame. *There were no fish*." Ibid.

[19] GM I, §17. "Must the ancient fire [of the greatest of all conflicts of ideals] not some day flare up much more terribly, after much longer preparation? More: must one not desire it with all one's might? even will it? even promote it?" Ibid.

[20] EH-GM.

21 EH-D, §2.
22 GM, Preface, §6.
23 EH-TI, §1.
24 EH-TI, §2.
25 TI, Foreword.
26 See chap. 2, sect. B, subsect. 1, above.
27 EH-TI, §1.
28 TI, Foreword. "One has renounced *grand* life when one renounces war." TI V, §3.
29 TI VI, §2. "There is no more dangerous error than that of *mistaking the consequence for the cause*: I call it reason's intrinsic form of corruption. Nonetheless, this error is among the most ancient and most recent habits of mankind: it is even sanctified among us, it bears the names 'religion' and 'morality.' *Every* proposition formulated by religion and morality contains it; priests and moral legislators are the authors of this corruption of reason." TI VI, §1. See also WP, §334.
30 EH-TI, §3. A year earlier, Nietzsche called this planned book *The Will to Power: Attempt at a Revaluation of All Values*. GM III, §27.
31 A, §13.
32 A, §62. Nietzsche completed *The Anti-Christ* – "the first book of the *Revaluation of all Values*" – on 30 September 1888, the day he wrote the foreword to the already-completed *Twilight of the Idols*. TI, Foreword.
33 About a month after completing *The Anti-Christ*, Nietzsche decided that his planned four-volume work would now consist of only *The Anti-Christ*. Young, *Nietzsche*, 541-42.
34 EH-TI, §3.
35 EH-CW, §4.
36 EH, Preface, §1. Contrary to Nietzsche's intent, *The Anti-Christ* was published in 1895 and *Ecce Homo* in 1908. In a letter to a friend on 30 October 1888, Nietzsche mentioned his commencement of writing *Ecce Homo* and then wrote, "Not only did I want to present myself *before* the uncannily solitary act of transvaluation; I would also just like to *test* what risks I can take with the German ideas of freedom of speech. My suspicion is that the *first* book of the revaluation will be confiscated on the spot – legally and in all justice." Friedrich Nietzsche, *Selected Letters of Friedrich Nietzsche*, ed. and trans. Christopher Middleton (Indianapolis: Hackett Publishing Company, 1996), 319.
37 EH-D, §2. Kaufmann's translation has been modified. See n. 3 on p. 36 above.
38 Ibid.
39 EH-BT, §4. Kaufmann's translation has been modified. He translated "Jene neue Partei des Lebens, welche die grösste aller Aufgaben, die Höherzüchtung der Menschheit in die Hände nimmt" as "That new party of life which would tackle the greatest of all tasks, the attempt to raise humanity higher." "Attempt" is not in the German sentence and "to raise humanity higher" does not express the biological denotation of *Höherzüchtung*. *Höher* means higher, *Langenscheidt*, s.v. "höher," and *Züchtung* means the "breeding" of animals, the "keeping" of bees, or the "growing" of plants. Ibid., s.v. "Züchtung." The translation of *Höherzüchtung der Menshheit* as

the "higher breeding of humanity" is not unusual. In his book about Nietzsche's Darwinism, Richardson translated this sentence as: "that new party of life, which takes in its hands the greatest of all tasks, the breeding higher of humanity." John Richardson, *Nietzsche's New Darwinism* (Oxford: Oxford University Press, 2008), 190. See also Steven E. Aschheim, *The Nietzsche Legacy in Germany: 1890-1990* (Berkeley: University of California Press, 1992), 326, where *die Höherzüchtung der Menschheit* is translated as "the higher breeding of humanity."
[40] See chap. 5, sects. D and E, below.
[41] EH-BT, §4.

Chapter 4

THUS SPOKE ZARATHUSTRA

In the preface to *Ecce Homo*, Nietzsche mentioned *Thus Spoke Zarathustra* as the one book of his which "stands to my mind by itself" and claimed that with it he has "given mankind the greatest present that has ever been made to it so far." This book "is not only the highest book there is, [. . .] it is also the *deepest*, born out of the innermost wealth of truth."[1] He also described *Zarathustra* as the product of almost revelatory inspiration[2] and called it the "profoundest book" humanity possesses.[3]

Despite the high self-praise, Nietzsche insisted that no "prophet" is speaking in this book, nor one of "those gruesome hybrids of sickness and will to power whom people call founders of religions. [. . .] It is no fanatic that speaks here; this is not 'preaching'; no *faith* is demanded here."[4] In this same section, however, he quoted *Zarathustra* to emphasize its historical importance: "It is the stillest words that bring on the storm. Thoughts that come on doves' feet guide the world."[5] He also later called Zarathustra "one who first *creates* truth, a *world-governing* spirit, a destiny."[6]

Regardless of his seemingly inconsistent characterizations of his book, Nietzsche solved the "Yes-saying part"[7] of his task in *Zarathustra* with "the idea of the eternal recurrence, this highest formula of affirmation that is at all attainable." Although the Overman (*der Übermensch*) is the best known concept in the book, he described the idea of the eternal recurrence (*der Ewige-Wiederkunfts-Gedanke*) as the "fundamental conception" and "basic idea"[8] of *Zarathustra* as well as the "doctrine of Zarathustra."[9]

During the course of the book, Zarathustra is transformed from being merely a herald of the Overman to being the Overman himself. He becomes the Overman by overcoming humanity, more specifically his nausea of humanity. He overcomes his nausea of humanity by willing the eternal recurrence of all things, even of the smallest man. As the Overman, Zarathustra teaches the doctrine of the eternal recurrence as the foundational idea of a new era that commences at an event called the Great Noon.[10] Essential characteristics of this new era are Zarathustra's new values of a new nobility (*einer neue Adel*) and its task of the higher breeding of humanity.

A. First Part

The first part of *Zarathustra* presents the teaching that the Overman is the "meaning of the earth"[11] and that Zarathustra is a "herald" of the Overman.[12] After ten years of solitude in the mountains, Zarathustra discovers a new "meaning of the earth" – the Overman – in response to humanity's loss of its supernatural meaning of life caused by the death of the Christian god. He descends the mountain to bring humanity a "gift"[13] of this new, but natural, meaning of the earth to replace the dead Christian god. The gift has a natural meaning because it is *"faithful to the earth"* and not based on "otherworldly hopes."[14]

As a "herald" of the Overman, Zarathustra does not teach the people that they should become the Overman but rather that humanity should set the Overman as its "goal" and "highest hope," the latter of which is henceforth used in *Zarathustra*, along with "the meaning of the earth," as a euphemism for the Overman. Zarathustra also warns that if humanity does not do this soon, the coming of "the *last man*" will forever preclude the appearance of the Overman.[15]

After his attempt to teach the people fails, Zarathustra seeks "companions" who can become fellow creators of the new values that contribute to the appearance of the Overman. Zarathustra's remaining speeches in the first part are his attempt to attract these companions. He wants to "lure many away from the herd" and its "shepherds."[16] Zarathustra's speeches teach both the "possibility" and "desirability" of the Overman.[17]

The first part ends with Zarathustra's parting from his newly acquired companions, now called his "disciples,"[18] and his return to solitude in his mountain cave. The teaching of the Overman as the meaning of the earth is now the responsibility of the disciples. Their task is to carry Zarathustra's teaching further in order to prepare the way for the Overman.[19]

In his farewell speech to his disciples, Zarathustra admonishes them to remain faithful to the earth and serve the meaning of the earth – the Overman.[20] He also bids his disciples to lose him and find themselves and only after they have all denied him will he return to them. He then predicts that he will be with his disciples "the third time" in order to "celebrate the great noon" together.[21] Zarathustra is with his disciples for the first time at the end of the first part and then for the second time in the second part of the book while upon the blessed isles. He returns to his solitude at the end of the second part. The third time that he is with his disciples, who are then called his "children," is at the end of the fourth part after receiving the sign that his children are near, his hour has come, and the Great Noon is imminent.[22]

The Great Noon is described in the first part as the point in human history "when man stands in the middle of his way between beast and overman and celebrates his way to the evening as his highest hope [i.e., the Overman]: for it is the way to a new morning." The "last will" of Zarathustra and his children on that Great Noon is the following: "*Dead are all gods: now we want the overman to live.*"[23] Announced here for the first time as a promise to his disciples, the Great Noon appears later in the third part[24] as a threat to those who are not his disciples before appearing for the last time at the end of the fourth part.[25]

B. Second Part

In the second part, Zarathustra learns the limitations of disciples and loses faith in the ability of disciples to improve on his work. He realizes that the task he has assigned to his disciples is his task. No longer wholly a teacher, Zarathustra becomes once again a learner.[26] He learns that the fundamental phenomenon of life is "the will to power,"[27] that "the most spiritual will to power"[28] is philosophy or "wisdom," which has hitherto been in the service of revenge,[29] and that the "bridge to the highest hope" (i.e., the Overman) is "*that man be delivered from revenge.*"[30] Deliverance from revenge through redemption (*die Erlösung*) becomes Zarathustra's new task.

41

Although the will is "the name of the liberator and joy-bringer," it is "still a prisoner." The will is a prisoner of "it was" – the past that cannot be changed. Because the will cannot change "that which was," it wreaks revenge on all who can suffer for its inability to go backwards. Revenge is "the will's ill will against time and its 'it was.'"[31]

To be delivered from revenge, one must attain redemption. Zarathustra's new definition of redemption is: "To redeem those who lived in the past and to re-create all 'it was' into a 'thus I willed it.'" To attain redemption, he teaches that the "will is a creator." "All 'it was' is a fragment, a riddle, a dreadful accident – until the creative will says to it, 'But thus I willed it.' Until the creative will says to it, 'But thus I will it; thus shall I will it.'"[32]

This creative will is the will to power as an agent of redemption. The will to power as avenger becomes the will to power as redeemer when the creative will wills the eternal recurrence of all things.[33] In other words, when willing the eternal recurrence of all things, the creative will "neither repents of the past nor rejects it nor takes revenge on it; rather, it rejoices in the whole of the past and wills it just as it is."[34]

In discussing *Zarathustra* in *Ecce Homo*, Nietzsche defined his task as the same as Zarathustra's and its meaning, according to Nietzsche, is unmistakable: Zarathustra "says Yes to the point of justifying, of redeeming even all of the past."[35] Adding the emphasis, Nietzsche then quoted *Zarathustra* where Zarathustra strictly defines his task.

> "I walk among men as among the fragments of the future – that future which I envisage. And this is all my creating and striving, that I create and carry together into One what is fragment and riddle and dreadful accident. And how could I bear to be a man if man were not also a creator and guesser of riddles and redeemer of accidents? *To redeem those who lived in the past* and to turn every 'it was' into a 'thus I willed it' – that alone should I call redemption."[36]

The Yes-saying part of the personal aspect of Nietzsche's task of a revaluation of all values is thus solved by the application of the idea of the eternal recurrence to this new definition of redemption. Eternal recurrence is the idea with which the most spiritual will to power overcomes the spirit of revenge and attains redemption.[37]

Although Zarathustra knows what must be done to attain redemption, he is not yet ready to perform that act of will.[38] At the end of the second part, Zarathustra leaves his disciples on the blessed isles to return to his solitude and thus abandons his role as herald of the Overman.

C. Third Part

Zarathustra, a herald of the Overman in the first part, becomes the one heralded in the third part. Although the making of disciples who will prepare the way for the Overman is no longer his goal, Zarathustra continues to have the goal of realizing the Overman. His act of sailing away from the blessed isles at the beginning of the third part demonstrates his willingness to undertake this goal himself.[39] He abandons his disciples in order to take the path called "impossibility," which is his "way to greatness,"[40] that is, the way of the Overman. Zarathustra achieves his goal of becoming the Overman when he attains redemption by willing the eternal recurrence of all things.

On the ship on which he embarked to depart the blessed isles, Zarathustra tells his fellow passengers a riddle that he saw, called "the vision of the loneliest." The "spirit of gravity," his "devil and archenemy," in the form of a dwarf, sat oppressively on his back dripping "leaden thoughts" into his brain. Mustering his courage – "courage which attacks: which slays even death itself, for it says, 'Was *that* life? Well then! Once more!'"[41] – Zarathustra describes to the dwarf his "abysmal thought" in the most descriptive presentation of the idea of the eternal recurrence in Nietzsche's books.[42]

After this presentation, the dwarf suddenly disappears from Zarathustra's vision, but he hears a dog howling and then sees a young shepherd gagging with a heavy black snake hanging out of his mouth. Zarathustra could not tear the snake out of the shepherd's throat so he cried, "Bite its head off!" The shepherd bit the snake's head off and jumped up. He was "no longer human" and laughs in a manner "that was no human laughter." Zarathustra longs for this laughter. This part of the vision of the loneliest is "a foreseeing"[43] or premonition of what happens to Zarathustra when he attains redemption.

At this point, however, Zarathustra is still not ready to summon his abysmal thought. He next realizes that the companions he once sought are not to be found "unless he first created them himself." No longer using the term "disciples," Zarathustra now calls his companions "my children." For "his children's sake, Zarathustra must perfect himself." In other words, he must attain redemption. After being "known and tested," each of Zarathustra's children will be his "companion," "fellow creator," and "fellow celebrant" who writes Zarathustra's will on Zarathustra's tablets "to contribute to the greater perfection of all things." But first Zarathustra must face his own "final testing and knowledge."[44]

As Zarathustra sits and waits in solitude for his own redemption and for the sign ("the laughing lion with the flock of doves") that the hour has come to go among humanity once more, he is "surrounded by broken tablets and new tablets half covered with writing."[45] Called "that decisive passage"[46] in *Ecce Homo*, "On Old and New Tablets" is the longest section in the book and contains Zarathustra's final weighing of the world before his redemption.[47] He summarizes some of his earlier teachings, breaks old tablets, and writes new values on new tablets while leaving half of the new tablets blank. The newly created values include a "new nobility" and the exhortation to "become hard" in order to create the new nobility, both of which will be discussed in the next chapter. He also repeats his earlier teaching on the higher breeding of humanity: "You shall not only reproduce yourself, but produce something higher."[48] At the end of this section, Zarathustra bids his will to save him for "a great destiny" so that he "may one day be ready and ripe in the great noon" and thus achieve "a great victory."[49] Zarathustra is now ready for his own redemption.

In the section called "The Convalescent," Zarathustra summons his "most abysmal thought"[50] – the idea of the eternal recurrence. After this summoning, he falls down and remains lying for seven days. As in the "vision of the loneliest," a monster crawls down Zarathustra's throat and suffocates him, but he bites off its head and spews it out. Thereby, Zarathustra attains redemption. Although redeemed, he is still sick from his own redemption. Zarathustra's animals call him the "convalescent" and tell him that his "great destiny" now is to be the *"teacher of the eternal recurrence."*[51]

The meaning of Zarathustra's "convalescence" can be found in *The Gay Science* where Nietzsche noted that the last words of the dying Socrates were: "O Crito, I owe Asclepius a rooster." As Asclepius was the god of medicine, these words meant: "O Crito, *life is a disease.*" The rooster was meant as a sacrifice because Socrates had been cured of a disease. Nietzsche concluded that "Socrates, Socrates *suffered life!*" He suffered life like a sickness. Therefore, "we must overcome even the Greeks!"[52] As the "Convalescent," Zarathustra is convalescing from the opinion that to live "means to be a long time sick." This opinion is consistent with the "wisest" of "every age" who, like Socrates, "have passed the identical judgment on life: *it is worthless.*"[53]

After his redemption and a private conversation with his re-deemed soul, Zarathustra speaks and dances with personified Life, which is followed by the marriage song of Zarathustra and Life in which she is given a new name, Eternity.[54] The "seal" of Zarathustra's perfection occurs in "The Seven Seals,"[55] the final section of the third part, when Zarathustra consummates his marriage to Life/Eternity and produces the children with whom he resumes his work to bring about the Great Noon.[56] Although Zarathustra's act of willing the eternal recurrence of all things is the foundational act of a new teaching that is liberated from the spirit of revenge and that is faithful to the earth, he must descend to humanity again, but this time as a legislator or commander, to implement the political consequences of his doctrine of the eternal recurrence.[57]

Thus ends the third part. Months and years pass by before the beginning of the fourth and last part.

D. Fourth and Last Part

In the first, second, and third parts, Zarathustra achieved his happiness by attaining redemption through the willing of the eternal recurrence of all things. The fourth part is an interlude between Zarathustra's attainment of redemption and the resumption of his work that will bring about the event called the Great Noon.[58] During this interlude, Zarathustra's work is jeopardized by pity, his final sin.

Months and years pass by after Zarathustra's redemption. From his cave in the mountains, he casts his "golden fishing rod" into the "human sea," but the "human fish" must come up to him because he still waits for the sign that the time has come for his descent.

> I, however, and my destiny – we do not speak to the Today, nor do we speak to the Never; we have patience and time and overmuch time in which to speak. For one day it must yet come and may not pass. What must come one day and may not pass? Our great *Hazar*: that is, our great distant human kingdom, the Zarathustra kingdom of a thousand years. How distant may this "distant" be? What is that to me? But for all that, this is no less certain: with both feet I stand firmly on this ground, on eternal ground, on hard primeval rock, on this highest, hardest, primeval mountain range to which all winds come as to the "weather-shed" and ask: where? and whence? and whither?[59]

While he is patiently waiting for his sign ("the laughing lion with the flock of doves"[60]), Zarathustra is tempted by pity for the higher men[61] who are caught by his "golden fishing rod." His encounters with these higher men jeopardize his work if he should yield to the temptation represented by these superior men of his age.[62] In *Ecce Homo*, Nietzsche wrote,

> The overcoming of pity I count among the *noble* virtues: as "Zarathustra's temptation" I invented a situation in which a great cry of distress reaches him, as pity tries to attack him like a final sin that would entice him away from *himself*. To remain the master at this point, to keep the eminence of one's task undefiled by the many lower and more myopic impulses that are at work in so-called selfless actions, that is the test, perhaps the ultimate test, which a Zarathustra must pass – his real *proof* of strength.[63]

The cry of distress comes from the "higher men," but these men are not Zarathustra's "proper companions. It is not for them that I wait here in my mountains. I want to go to my work, to my day. [. . .] But I still lack the right men."[64] He waits "for those who are higher, stronger, more triumphant, and more cheerful, such as are built perpendicular in body and soul: *laughing lions* must come!"[65] These laughing lions Zarathustra later describes as "the lords of the earth," who are the "purest" and "the most unknown, the strongest, the midnight souls who are brighter and deeper than any day."[66]

Suddenly, Zarathustra is surrounded by flying doves and a lion appears at his feet. "*The sign is at hand,*" says Zarathustra. "*My children are near, my children.*"[67] When the higher men awake and start coming out of Zarathustra's cave, the lion roars at them and scares them back into the cave. Zarathustra remembers that the soothsayer (one of the higher men) prophesied the higher men's cry of distress by which the soothsayer wanted to seduce and tempt Zarathustra to his final sin (i.e., pity for the higher man). Zarathustra responds,

"Well then, *that* has had its time! My suffering and my pity for suffering – what does it matter! Am I concerned with *happiness*? I am concerned with my *work*.

"Well then! The lion came, my children are near, Zarathustra has ripened, my hour has come: this is *my* morning, *my* day is breaking: *rise now, rise, thou great noon!*"[68]

Thus ends the fourth part and begins Zarathustra's resumption of his work in the morning of a metaphorical day that will culminate in the event called the Great Noon. For Zarathustra, the Great Noon will be "a great destiny" and "a great victory,"[69] which requires that he bring his "richest gift"[70] – his perfected, redeemed, "ripened" soul – and the means to it – the teaching of the eternal recurrence – to his children who, after being "known and tested," will be Zarathustra's fellow creators in contributing "to the greater perfection of all things" by writing Zarathustra's will on Zarathustra's tablets such new values as the new nobility and its task of the higher breeding of humanity.[71] As discussed earlier,[72] the Great Noon is that event at which the most elect (i.e., Zarathustra's children) answer the questions of Why? and For What? by consecrating themselves to the task of the higher breeding of humanity. The Great Noon will then eventually usher in the "great *Hazar* [. . .] the Zarathustra kingdom of a thousand years."[73]

47

Before continuing our discussion of Zarathustra's new values in chapter 5, we shall more fully explain Nietzsche's concept of the Overman and the idea of the eternal recurrence.

E. Overman

Nietzsche used the word "Overman" (*der Übermensch*) to designate Zarathustra's "supreme achievement"[74] of attaining redemption through the willing of the eternal recurrence of all things. Redemption requires the overcoming of humanity, which means overcoming one's nausea over humanity. Contrary to a common misunderstanding, the Overman is not a product of biological evolution because the concept of the Overman, according to Nietzsche, has already become the "greatest reality"[75] in Zarathustra.

In *Ecce Homo*, Nietzsche explained that he used the word Overman in *Zarathustra* "as the designation of a type of supreme achievement, as opposed to 'modern' men, to 'good' men, to Christians and other nihilists." At the same time, he complained that the word has been misunderstood "as an 'idealistic' type of a higher kind of man, half 'saint,' half 'genius,'" the opposite of those very values that Nietzsche meant Zarathustra, "the annihilator of morality," to represent.[76]

Nietzsche also complained that other "scholarly oxen" have even suspected him of "Darwinism."[77] This mistake is understandable when considering how the concept of the Overman was introduced in *Zarathustra*. In the prologue, Zarathustra begins his speech to the people in the market place with these words:

> "*I teach you the overman.* Man is something that shall be overcome. What have you done to overcome him?
>
> "All beings so far have created something beyond themselves; and do you want to be the ebb of this great flood and even go back to the beasts rather than overcome man? What is the ape to man? A laughingstock or a painful embarrassment. And man shall be just that for the overman: a laughingstock or a painful embarrassment. You have made your way from worm to man, and much in you is still worm. Once you were apes, and even now, too, man is more ape than any ape."[78]

Later, Zarathustra places humanity between the beast and the Overman. "Man is a rope, tied between beast and overman – a rope over an abyss." Humanity is "not an end" but a "bridge" between beast and Overman.[79] This language implies that the Overman is the meaning of the earth because he is the end of the evolutionary process, of which humanity is just a bridge and toward which humanity must now consciously strive.[80]

Yet, the concept of the Overman cannot be conceived as an evolutionary step beyond humanity because Zarathustra later becomes the Overman himself. Although Nietzsche arguably presents the Overman as an evolutionary phenomenon in the prologue and the first part, this image is subsequently replaced by the transformation of Zarathustra into the Overman.[81] Zarathustra himself becomes the Overman. Also, Zarathustra always expresses the term Overman in the singular. He is not the herald of Over*men* who develop into a new species that will collectively replace the human species.[82]

What then is the Overman? Simply, the Overman is one who has overcome (*überwinden*) humanity. In the sentence immediately after introducing the Overman, Zarathustra says, "Man is something that shall be overcome."[83] He repeats this expression or something similar to it in several places throughout the book.[84] For example, Zarathustra teaches that the warriors' "highest hope" (i.e., the Overman) and "highest thought of life" shall be that "man is something that shall be overcome."[85] Most revealingly, Zarathustra explains in his speech to the "higher men" in the fourth part that he was "the first and only one to ask: 'How is man to be overcome?' I have the overman at heart, *that* is my first and only concern – and *not* man."[86]

Furthermore, in *Ecce Homo*, Nietzsche explained that in Zarathustra "man has been overcome at every moment; the concept of the 'overman' has here become the greatest reality – whatever was so far considered great in man lies beneath him at an infinite distance."[87] In other words, the concept of the Overman became the greatest reality in Zarathustra when he overcame humanity.

Zarathustra overcomes humanity to become the Overman by overcoming his nausea over humanity. He also uses the words "contempt" and "disgust" to describe this nausea. In the prologue, Zarathustra describes the Overman as the "sea" in which one's "great contempt can go under." The "greatest experience" one can have is "the hour of the great contempt" in which one's happiness, reason, and virtue arouse one's "disgust" because they are "poverty and filth and wretched contentment."[88]

When Zarathustra overcomes his nausea over humanity by willing the eternal recurrence of all things, he attains redemption and becomes the Overman. In the "vision of the loneliest,"[89] a premonition of Zarathustra's own redemption, the young shepherd gags with a heavy black snake hanging out of his mouth. There is "much nausea and pale dread" in his face. With Zarathustra's cry to bite its head off, his own "dread," "hatred," "nausea," "pity," and "all that is good and wicked" in him cried out of him with "a single cry."[90]

During his own redemption, Zarathustra summons his "most abysmal thought" – the idea of the eternal recurrence – and as it appears, he says, just before falling down as one dead, "Nausea, nausea, nausea – woe unto me!"[91] After waking up and resting for seven days, he tells his animals what had happened. Zarathustra's "great disgust" with humanity was what had crawled into his throat in the form of a monster and choked him. His disgust with all existence was caused by the eternal recurrence of all things, even of the smallest man. "Naked I had once seen both, the greatest man and the smallest man: all-too-similar to each other, even the greatest all-too-human. All-too-small, the greatest! – that was my disgust with man. And the eternal recurrence even of the smallest – that was my disgust with all existence. Alas! Nausea! Nausea! Nausea!"[92]

For the remainder of the book, Zarathustra is the redeemed one because he has overcome his nausea over humanity by willing the eternal recurrence of all things. In the fourth part, upon recognizing who is with him, the voluntary beggar (one of the higher men) says, "This is the man without nausea, this is Zarathustra himself, the man who overcame the great nausea; this is the eye, this is the mouth, this is the heart of Zarathustra himself."[93] The overcoming of this "great nausea" through the willing of the eternal recurrence of all things was Zarathustra's "supreme achievement."[94]

Nietzsche continued the theme of Zarathustra's overcoming of his nausea of humanity in *Ecce Homo*. In the last section on *Zarathustra*, Nietzsche explained how, now that Zarathustra has become the Overman by mastering "the *great nausea* over man," humanity is for him an "ugly stone" that needs a "sculptor" with a hard hammer to create more Overmen out of it.

> In another passage he [i.e., Zarathustra] defines as strictly as possible what alone "man" can be for him – *not* an object of love or, worse, pity – Zarathustra has mastered the *great nausea* over man, too: man is for him an un-form, a material, an ugly stone that needs a sculptor.
> "*Willing* no more and *esteeming* no more and *creating* no more – oh, that this great weariness might always remain far from me! In knowledge, too, I feel only my will's joy in begetting and becoming; and if there is innocence in my knowledge, it is because the *will to beget* is in it. Away from God and gods this will has lured me; what could one create if gods – were there?
> "But my fervent will to create impels me ever again toward man; thus is the hammer impelled toward the stone. O men, in the stone an image is sleeping, the image of images! Alas, that it has to sleep in the hardest, ugliest stone! *Now my hammer rages cruelly against its prison.* Pieces of rock rain from the stone: what is that to me? I want to perfect it; for a shadow came to me – the stillest and lightest of all things once came to me. The beauty of the overman came to me as a shadow. O my brothers, what are gods to me now?"
> I stress a final point: the verse in italics furnishes the occasion. Among the conditions for a *Dionysian* task are, in a decisive way, the hardness of the hammer, the *joy even in destroying.* The imperative, "become hard!" the most fundamental certainty *that all creators are hard*, is the distinctive mark of a Dionysian nature.[95]

Although the Overman already, Zarathustra wants to become a "sculptor" in order to create more Overmen with his hard hammer out of the "ugly stone" called humanity. This Dionysian[96] task requires the creator to be hard, even in destroying. In addition to being hard, a Dionysian nature is characterized by the idea of the eternal recurrence.

51

F. Eternal Recurrence

As mentioned earlier,[97] Nietzsche solved the "Yes-saying part" of his task with the idea of the eternal recurrence (*der Ewige-Wiederkunfts-Gedanke*), the "highest formula of affirmation that is at all attainable."[98] It is an ethical or moral principle, not a scientific or metaphysical principle.[99] Although the idea of the eternal recurrence is only described fully twice in his books, once as a thought experiment involving a demon and the other as one of Zarathustra's visions, Nietzsche considered this principle one of his most important philosophical ideas.[100] At the end of *Twilight of the Idols*, Nietzsche called himself "the teacher of the eternal recurrence,"[101] just as Zarathustra's animals call Zarathustra *"the teacher of the eternal recurrence"*[102] after his redemption.

In relating the history of *Zarathustra*, Nietzsche revealed that the "fundamental conception of this work, the idea of the eternal recurrence [. . .] belongs in August 1881."[103] He wrote the first edition of *The Gay Science* (1882) in the interval between the coming of the idea of the eternal recurrence in August 1881 and the beginning of the writing of *Zarathustra* in 1883.

The first edition of *The Gay Science* offers the first expression of the idea of the eternal recurrence, "the basic idea of *Zarathustra*,"[104] in the penultimate section of the fourth book (the last book of the first edition), which was followed by the section[105] containing "the beginning of *Zarathustra*."[106]

> *The greatest weight.* – What, if some day or night a demon were to steal after you into your loneliest loneliness and say to you: "This life as you now live it and have lived it, you will have to live once more and innumerable times more; and there will be nothing new in it, but every pain and every joy and every thought and sigh and everything unutterably small or great in your life will have to return to you, all in the same succession and sequence – even this spider and this moonlight between the trees, and even this moment and I myself. The eternal hourglass of existence is turned upside down again and again, and you with it, speck of dust!"

Would you not throw yourself down and gnash your teeth and curse the demon who spoke thus? Or have you once experienced a tremendous moment when you would have answered him: "You are a god and never have I heard anything more divine." If this thought gained possession of you, it would change you as you are or perhaps crush you. The question in each and every thing, "Do you desire this once more and innumerable times more?" would lie upon your actions as the greatest weight. Or how well disposed would you have to become to yourself and to life *to crave nothing more fervently* than this ultimate eternal confirmation and seal?[107]

In this thought experiment, Nietzsche challenged each of us to ask ourselves whether or not we would "curse the demon" who told us that we would have to live every moment of our lives over and over again for eternity. It could be a godsend. Or the question could crush us like a great weight or it could spur us to action. If we would "curse the demon," then perhaps the challenge would serve as a stimulus to our will to power to act in such a way that we shall eventually become well enough disposed to ourselves and to life to crave nothing more fervently than this eternal recurrence and to be able to say to death, "Was *that* life? Well then! Once more!"[108]

Nietzsche expressed the idea of the eternal recurrence quite differently in *Zarathustra*, although the spider and the moonlight are both present again. Zarathustra calls it his "abysmal thought" and describes it to the "spirit of gravity," his "devil and archenemy,"[109] who takes the form of a dwarf.

"Behold this gateway, dwarf!" I continued. "It has two faces. Two paths meet here; no one has yet followed either to its end. This long lane stretches back for an eternity. And the long lane out there, that is another eternity. They contradict each other, these paths; they offend each other face to face; and it is here at this gateway that they come together. The name of the gateway is inscribed above: 'Moment.' But whoever would follow one of them, on and on, farther and farther – do you believe, dwarf, that these paths contradict each other eternally?" [. . .]

"Behold," I continued, "this moment! From this gateway, Moment, a long, eternal lane leads *backward*: behind us lies an eternity. Must not whatever *can* walk have walked on this lane before? Must not whatever *can* happen have happened, have been done, have passed by before? And if everything has been there before – what do you think, dwarf, of this moment? Must not this gateway too have been there before? And are not all things knotted together so firmly that this moment draws after it *all* that is to come? Therefore – itself too? For whatever *can* walk – in this long lane out *there* too, it *must* walk once more.

"And this slow spider, which crawls in the moonlight, and this moonlight itself, and I and you in the gateway, whispering together, whispering of eternal things – must not all of us have been there before? And return and walk in that other lane, out there, before us, in this long dreadful lane – must we not eternally return?"[110]

This is the "abysmal thought" that Zarathustra must first summon before he can overcome his nausea of humanity and attain redemption.

After this description in *Zarathustra*, Nietzsche did not explicitly discuss or describe the idea of the eternal recurrence in his next books, *Beyond Good and Evil*, *On the Genealogy of Morals*, and *The Case of Wagner*, but in *Twilight of the Idols* and *Ecce Homo*, he implied or suggested how important the doctrine was to him without formulating it, except briefly once.[111] As the "doctrine of Zarathustra," Nietzsche succinctly described the "doctrine of the 'eternal recurrence'" in *Ecce Homo* as "the unconditional and infinitely repeated circular course of all things."[112]

Despite the relatively few times that the idea of the eternal recurrence is discussed or described, it is one of Nietzsche's most important ideas. Its importance lies in its relationship with the spirit of gravity. Not only did Zarathustra attain his own redemption through the willing of the eternal recurrence of all things, he also achieved a "great victory"[113] over the "spirit of gravity." Zarathustra calls "the spirit of gravity, my supreme and most powerful devil, of whom they say that he is 'the master of the world.'"[114] The spirit of gravity represents Plato and all forms of Platonism, such as Christianity and its heir, the democratic enlightenment, that have mastered the world.[115]

In the preface of his next book, *Beyond Good and Evil*, Nietzsche provided another explanation of the enemy that he called the "spirit of gravity" in *Zarathustra*. The enemy is Plato and his dogmatic philosophy called Platonism, which contains "the worst, most durable, and most dangerous of all errors so far [. . .] a dogmatist's error – namely, Plato's invention of the pure spirit and the good as such."[116] Plato wanted "to prove to himself that reason and instinct of themselves tend toward one goal, the good, 'God.' And since Plato, all theologians and philosophers are on the same track – that is, in moral matters it has so far been instinct, or what the Christians call 'faith,' or 'the herd,' as I put it, that has triumphed."[117] The "Christian faith [. . .] was also the faith of Plato, that God is the truth, that truth is divine."[118] Therefore, the enemy is also Christianity, which is simply "Platonism for 'the people.'"[119]

With his victory over the spirit of gravity, Zarathustra overcame not only the Greeks,[120] but the whole Platonic tradition, to include Christianity and the democratic enlightenment. By doing so, he also achieved a victory over slave morality and in the process provided the basis for a new master morality. The idea of the eternal recurrence replaces Platonism in all its forms with a new center of gravity that is liberated from the spirit of revenge and that is faithful to the earth.[121] With this new center of gravity, Nietzsche could now give a new weight to things.[122] In this way, the idea of the eternal recurrence provides the basis of Nietzsche's philosophy of the future.

---

[1] EH, Preface, §4.
[2] EH-Z, §3.
[3] TI IX, §51.
[4] EH, Preface, §4.
[5] Ibid. (quoting Z II, The Stillest Hour).
[6] EH-Z, §6.
[7] EH-BGE, §1.
[8] EH-Z, §1.
[9] EH-BT, §3.
[10] This Great Noon is the same Great Noon that Nietzsche described in *Ecce Homo*.

See chap. 3 above.

[11] Z I, Prologue, §3.

[12] Z I, Prologue, §4.

[13] Z I, Prologue, §2.

[14] Z I, Prologue, §3.

[15] Z I, Prologue, §5.

[16] Z I, Prologue, §9.

[17] Lampert, *Nietzsche's Teaching*, 32.

[18] Z I, On the Gift-Giving Virtue, §1.

[19] Lampert, *Nietzsche's Teaching*, 73.

[20] Z I, On the Gift-Giving Virtue, §2.

[21] Z I, On the Gift-Giving Virtue, §3.

[22] Z IV, The Sign.

[23] Z I, On the Gift-Giving Virtue, §3.

[24] Z III, On Virtue That Makes Small, §3; Z III, On Passing By; Z III, On the Three Evils, §2.

[25] Z IV, The Sign.

[26] Lampert, *Nietzsche's Teaching*, 80-81.

[27] Z II, On Self-Overcoming.

[28] BGE, §9.

[29] Lampert, *Nietzsche's Teaching*, 140.

[30] Z II, On the Tarantulas.

[31] Z II, On Redemption.

[32] Ibid.

[33] Lampert, *Nietzsche's Teaching*, 147.

[34] Ibid., 149.

[35] EH-Z, §8.

[36] Ibid. (quoting Z II, On Redemption).

[37] Lampert, *Nietzsche's Teaching*, 140.

[38] Z II, The Stillest Hour.

[39] Lampert, *Nietzsche's Teaching*, 83-84.

[40] Z III, The Wanderer.

[41] Z III, On the Vision and the Riddle, §1.

[42] Z III, On the Vision and the Riddle, §2. For the presentation, see chap. 4, sect. F, below.

[43] Ibid.

[44] Z III, On Involuntary Bliss.

[45] Z III, On Old and New Tablets, §1.

[46] EH-Z, §4.

[47] Lampert, *Nietzsche's Teaching*, 203.

[48] Z I, On Child and Marriage. See also Z III, On Old and New Tablets, §24.

[49] Z III, On Old and New Tablets, §30.

[50] Z III, The Convalescent, §1.

[51] Z III, The Convalescent, §2.

[52] GS, §340.

53 TI II, §1.
54 Lampert, *Nietzsche's Teaching*, 211.
55 Ibid., 173.
56 Ibid., 242.
57 Ibid., 157-58.
58 Ibid., 288.
59 Z IV, The Honey Sacrifice. "*Hazar* is the Persian word meaning millennium or thousand." One of Nietzsche's notes "speaks of the Persians as the first to have thought of history as a totality, a sequence of developments each presided over by a prophet whose *hazar*, or *Reich*, lasts a thousand years." Lampert, *Nietzsche's Teaching*, 354.
60 Z III, On Old and New Tablets, §1.
61 The "higher man" in the fourth part is not the Overman.
62 Lampert, *Nietzsche's Teaching*, 288.
63 EH I, §4.
64 Z IV, The Sign.
65 Z IV, The Welcome.
66 Z IV, The Drunken Song, §7.
67 Z IV, The Sign.
68 Ibid. The timing of the Great Noon as announced at the end of the first part has moved to the next day in the fourth part. No longer is the Great Noon "when man stands in the middle of his way between beast and overman." Z I, On the Gift-Giving Virtue, §3. Because Zarathustra already became the Overman, the Great Noon now occurs on the next day during "a new morning." Ibid. This "new morning" is Zarathustra's hour, morning, and day. Z IV, The Sign.
69 Z III, On Old and New Tablets, §30.
70 Z III, On Old and New Tablets, §3.
71 Z III, On Involuntary Bliss.
72 See chap. 3 above.
73 Z IV, The Honey Sacrifice.
74 EH III, §1.
75 EH-Z, §6.
76 EH III, §1.
77 Ibid. Despite his many critical comments of Charles Darwin's theory of evolution by natural selection, Nietzsche appropriated the central idea of the theory and attempted to extend or build beyond it, so much that one scholar has called Nietzsche's philosophy a "new Darwinism." Richardson, *Nietzsche's New Darwinism*, 4. By early 1873, Nietzsche had decided that Darwin's theory of evolution was something "I hold to be true." Young, *Nietzsche*, 179.
78 Z I, Prologue, §3.
79 Z I, Prologue, §4.
80 Lampert, *Nietzsche's Teaching*, 19.
81 Ibid., 20.
82 Ibid.
83 Z I, Prologue, §3.

84 Z I, On Enjoying and Suffering the Passions; Z I, On War and Warriors; Z I, On the Friend; Z III, On Old and New Tablets, §3; Z III, On Old and New Tablets, §4; Z IV, The Ugliest Man.

85 Z I, On War and Warriors.

86 Z IV, On the Higher Man, §3.

87 EH-Z, §6.

88 Z I, Prologue, §3.

89 Z III, On the Vision and the Riddle, §1. See chap. 4, sect. C, above.

90 Z III, On the Vision and the Riddle, §2.

91 Z III, The Convalescent, §1.

92 Z III, The Convalescent, §2.

93 Z IV, The Voluntary Beggar.

94 EH III, §1.

95 EH-Z, §8 (quoting Z II, Upon the Blessed Isles).

96 For a discussion of the concept of the Dionysian, see chap. 6 below.

97 See chap. 4, sect. B, above.

98 EH-Z, §1.

99 Although Nietzsche formulated some scientific proofs of the idea of the eternal recurrence in his notes, he never offered any of these proofs in his published books. *The Encyclopedia of Philosophy*, s.v. "Nietzsche, Friedrich."

100 Young, *Nietzsche*, 318. Nietzsche's word for recurrence or return, *Wiederkunft*, has a religious connotation. The "second coming" of Christ is called *die Wiederkunft Christi*. Ibid.

101 TI X, §5.

102 Z III, The Convalescent, §2.

103 EH-Z, §1. See cited text at n. 22 on pp. xvii-xviii above.

104 Ibid.

105 GS, §342. Except for a few words, this section is identical to the first section of Zarathustra's prologue.

106 EH-Z, §1.

107 GS, §341.

108 Z III, On the Vision and the Riddle, §1.

109 Ibid.

110 Z III, On the Vision and the Riddle, §2.

111 TI X, §5; EH-BT, §3; EH-Z, §1.

112 EH-BT, §3.

113 Z III, On Old and New Tablets, §30.

114 Z II, The Dancing Song.

115 Lampert, *Nietzsche's Teaching*, 198-99.

116 BGE, Preface.

117 BGE, §191.

118 GS, §344. "In the great fatality of Christianity, Plato is that ambiguity and fascination called the 'ideal' which made it possible for the nobler natures of antiquity to misunderstand themselves and to step on to the *bridge* which led to the 'Cross.'" TI X, §2.

[119] BGE, Preface.

[120] GS, §340. See chap. 4, sect. C, above. It is not coincidental that GS, §340, the last words of which are "we must overcome even the Greeks!" is followed by the first expression of the idea of the eternal recurrence in GS, §341, and the beginning of *Zarathustra* in GS, §342.

[121] Lampert, *Nietzsche's Teaching*, 193.

[122] Ibid., 197. "For it has been the proper task of all great thinkers to be lawgivers as to the measure, stamp and weight of things." UM III, §3. "*In what do you believe?* – In this, that the weights of all things must be determined anew." GS, §269.

Chapter 5

PHILOSOPHY OF THE FUTURE

Nietzsche's "philosophy of the future"[1] is a new master morality. The key concepts of Nietzsche's new philosophy include philosophical materialism as its ontological foundation, the "will to power" – the fundamental phenomenon of life – as its new standard of value, and "beyond good and evil" as the moral stance by which the philosophers of the future create the new values that the new nobility implements to tackle the task of the higher breeding of humanity. Like Zarathustra who only covers half of his new tablets of values with writing, Nietzsche provided only the essential elements of his new master morality. He called on "philosophers of the future" to complete it.

A. Remain Faithful to the Earth

Nietzsche was a philosophical materialist who recognized the existence of only material things with physical properties and only a naturalistic understanding of this reality.[2] In his mature work, he rejected metaphysical idealism.[3] He did not think that a metaphysical world, even if it existed, was knowable.[4] Also, he did not think that the meaning of life could be found in any transcendence of life or reality. Zarathustra, as Nietzsche's mouthpiece, expressed this materialism in his exhortation to *"remain faithful to the earth."*[5]

The earth to which Zarathustra commands faithfulness is the same earth that was regarded as merely the "apparent" world by those who believed in the "true" or "real" world invented by Plato. "The 'apparent' world is the only one: the 'real' world has only been *lyingly added*."⁶ "One has deprived reality of its value, its meaning, its truthfulness, to precisely the extent to which one has mendaciously invented an ideal world. The 'true world' and the 'apparent world' – that means: the mendaciously invented world and reality."⁷

Philosophically, *Thus Spoke Zarathustra* begins at the historical point at which the "real world" is abolished, but when the real world is abolished, the apparent world is also abolished. There is only one world left – the actual world. In his "History of an Error" in *Twilight of the Idols*, Nietzsche described the point when only the actual world was left as "Mid-day; moment of the shortest shadow; end of the longest error; zenith of mankind; INCIPIT ZARATHUSTRA ["Here begins Zarathustra"]."⁸ Consequently, *Zarathustra* begins with "a new conception of the meaning of the world."⁹

In *Zarathustra*, Nietzsche's materialism is expressed through Zarathustra who exhorts the people to "remain faithful to the earth" by making the Overman the meaning of the earth and not believing those who speak of "otherworldly hopes." With the death of the Christian god, to "sin against the earth is now the most dreadful thing, and to esteem the entrails of the unknowable higher than the meaning of the earth." This means that the earth is not to be disparaged by "otherworldly hopes."¹⁰

Although Zarathustra often speaks of the "soul" (*die Seele*), it is not an immortal soul, nor is it nonmaterial. In response to the tightrope walker's fear of going to hell, Zarathustra tells him that "there is no devil and no hell. Your soul will be dead even before your body: fear nothing further."¹¹ In his speech on the despisers of the body, Zarathustra says the "body am I entirely, and nothing else; and soul is only a word for something about the body."¹² Later, his animals have him say, "The soul is as mortal as the body."¹³

Nietzsche thought that the "great lie of personal immortality destroys all rationality, all naturalness of instinct – all that is salutary, all that is life-furthering, all that holds a guarantee of the future in the instincts henceforth excites mistrust."¹⁴ Furthermore, immortality "granted to every Peter and Paul has been the greatest and most malicious outrage on *noble* mankind ever committed."¹⁵

In his speech on the afterworldly, Zarathustra provides an explanation for the belief in such "otherworldly hopes" as an immortal soul.

He claims that it was "suffering and incapacity that created all after-worlds" and weariness "created all gods and afterworlds." "It was the sick and decaying who despised body and earth and invented the heavenly realm and the redemptive drops of blood."[16]

In an earlier book, Nietzsche provided a different, but still materialistic, explanation for the origin of metaphysics.

> The man of the ages of barbarous primordial culture believed that in the dream he was getting to know a *second real world*: here is the origin of all metaphysics. Without the dream one would have had no occasion to divide the world into two. The dissection into soul and body is also connected with the oldest idea of the dream, likewise the postulation of a life of the soul, thus the origin of all belief in spirits, and probably also of the belief in gods. "The dead live on, *for* they appear to the living in dreams": that was the conclusion one formerly drew, throughout many millennia.[17]

Nietzsche continued his critique of the Christian despisers of the body in a later book where he called "the ascetic ideal, the priests' ideal [. . .] the *harmful* ideal *par excellence*, a will to the end, an ideal of decadence,"[18] because of its effects upon health. "I know of hardly anything else that has had so destructive an effect upon the *health* and racial strength of Europeans as this [ascetic] ideal; one may without any exaggeration call it *the true calamity* in the history of European health."[19] Elsewhere, Nietzsche wrote, "Christianity, which despised the body, has up till now been mankind's greatest misfortune."[20]

As a materialist, Nietzsche strongly objected to the idealism of Christianity. As already discussed,[21] Christianity denaturalized nature and devalued natural values. After his first proclamation that "God is dead,"[22] Nietzsche listed several "shadows of God," such as laws of nature, which still have to be vanquished in the same way that God was vanquished. When we have vanquished the shadows of God, we shall complete the "de-deification of nature" and "begin to '*naturalize*' humanity in terms of a pure, newly discovered, newly redeemed nature."[23] Nietzsche later described that task as follows: "To translate man back into nature; to become master over the many vain and overly enthusiastic interpretations and connotations that have so far been scrawled and painted over that eternal basic text of *homo natura*."[24] Thus, Nietzsche taught "the dehumanization of nature and the naturalization of man."[25]

As part of his own faithfulness to the earth, Nietzsche emphasized the "basic concerns of life itself" like "nutrition, place, climate, recreation, the whole casuistry of selfishness" as being "inconceivably more important than everything one has taken to be important so far," such as "mere imaginings" like "God," "soul," "virtue," "sin," "beyond," "truth," and "eternal life," which are "*lies* prompted by the bad instincts of sick natures that were harmful in the most profound sense." Nietzsche devoted almost the whole chapter entitled "Why I Am So Clever" in *Ecce Homo* to these "little" things.[26] He objected to the Christian concepts of "soul," "spirit," and "*immortal* soul" because they were "invented in order to despise the body" and used to oppose "everything that deserves to be taken seriously in life, the questions of nourishment, abode, spiritual diet, treatment of the sick, cleanliness, and weather."[27]

In another example of his faithfulness to the earth, Nietzsche cited a proposition against vice from his moral code. He used the word "vice" in his fight against every kind of antinature or idealism. The proposition reads: "The preaching of chastity amounts to a public incitement to antinature. Every kind of contempt for sex, every impurification of it by means of the concept 'impure,' is the crime *par excellence* against life – is the real sin against the holy spirit of life."[28]

Finally, Nietzsche found no value in metaphysical idealism because it is a symptom of declining life in which the will to power is lacking. "To divide the world into a 'real' and an 'apparent' world, whether in the manner of Christianity or in the manner of Kant (which is, after all, that of a *cunning* Christian –) is only a suggestion of *décadence* – a symptom of *declining* life."[29] In contrast, Nietzsche found value in ascending life, which is a manifestation of the will to power.

B. Will to Power

With materialism as the ontological foundation of his philosophy of the future, Nietzsche examined the fundamental phenomenon of life and discovered it to be the will to power (*der Wille zur Macht*) because "life simply *is* will to power."[30] Power itself in its many forms, ascending life, and life affirmation are all manifestations of the will to power. In his new master morality, Nietzsche used the concept of the will to power and its various manifestations as his standard of value for a new order of rank among values.

Nietzsche first revealed his discovery of the will to power in *Zarathustra* when Zarathustra learns that the fundamental phenomenon of life is the "will to power." He calls it "the unexhausted procreative will of life." He also recognizes the "will to truth" as a manifestation of the will to power.[31]

Because "in all events a *will to power* is operating," Nietzsche perceived his concept of the will to power as the "essence of life."[32] The "essence" of the world is "will to power."[33] He proposed that "our entire instinctive life" is "the development and ramification of *one* basic form of the will – namely, of the will to power." All organic functions, including procreation and nourishment, can be traced back to this will to power. "The world viewed from inside, the world defined and determined according to its 'intelligible character' – it would be 'will to power' and nothing else."[34]

Nietzsche's conception of the will to power is different from the "instinct of self-preservation." The "instinct of self-preservation" is not "the cardinal instinct of an organic being. A living thing seeks above all to *discharge* its strength – life itself is *will to power*; self-preservation is only one of the indirect and most frequent *results*."[35]

The will to power is also different from Darwin's "struggle for existence" or "struggle for life." "The struggle for existence is only an *exception*, a temporary restriction of the will to life. The great and small struggle always revolves around superiority, around growth and expansion, around power – in accordance with the will to power which is the will of life."[36] Likewise, the struggle for life is the exception. The "general aspect of life is *not* hunger and distress, but rather wealth, luxury, even absurd prodigality – where there is a struggle it is a struggle for *power*."[37]

And the will to power is not the same as the will to existence. As Zarathustra expresses it, the "will to existence" does not exist. "For, what does not exist cannot will; but what is in existence, how could that still want existence? Only where there is life is there also will: not will to life but – thus I teach you – will to power."[38]

The will to power manifests itself in many forms. The use of physical force or exertion in a fight or sporting event is an obvious example of the manifestation of the will to power. A less obvious example is simply helping others. "Benefiting and hurting others are ways of exercising one's power upon others."[39]

Resisting any "sentimental weakness" and seeing life as it is, Nietzsche insisted that the exploitation of man by man is also a manifestation of the will to power and is, therefore, "the *primordial fact* of all history."[40]

> Here we must beware of superficiality and get to the bottom of the matter, resisting all sentimental weakness: life itself is *essentially* appropriation, injury, overpowering of what is alien and weaker; suppression, hardness, imposition of one's own forms, incorporation and at least, at its mildest, exploitation [. . .]
>
> [. . .] "Exploitation" does not belong to a corrupt or imperfect and primitive society: it belongs to the *essence* of what lives, as a basic organic function; it is a consequence of the will to power, which is after all the will of life.[41]

The will to power also has spiritual manifestations, such as the instinct for freedom[42] and the urge to philosophize. Philosophy is "the most spiritual will to power." As such, philosophy is "this tyrannical drive" to "the 'creation of the world,' to the *causa prima* ["first cause"]," which "always creates the world in its own image; it cannot do otherwise."[43] In other words, philosophy is the drive to rule the world through its interpretation and creation.[44]

The will to power also manifests itself in what Nietzsche called "ascending life." He contrasted the ascending life with declining life in which the will to power is lacking. He considered life itself to be "instinct for growth, for continuance, for accumulation of forces, for *power*: where the will to power is lacking there is decline."[45] Declining life is "the diminution of all organizing power, that is to say the power of separating, of opening up chasms, of ranking above and below."[46]

As "symptoms of declining life," Nietzsche listed "the advent of democracy, international courts in place of war, equal rights for women, [and] the religion of pity."[47]

Nietzsche equated decline with decadence. "Wherever the will to power declines in any form there is every time also a physiological regression, a *décadence*."[48] He developed several formulas or recipes for decadence, all involving the loss of the instinct of life in one form or another.[49] One of those formulas for decadence is "to *have* to combat one's instincts" because "as long as life is *ascending*, happiness and instinct are one."[50]

Nietzsche considered the natural value of a person's egoism to be dependent on whether that person represented the ascending or descending line of life.

> If he represents the ascending line his value is in fact extraordinary – and for the sake of the life-collective, which with him takes a step *forward*, the care expended on his preservation, on the creation of optimum conditions for him, may even be extreme. [. . .] If he represents the descending development, decay, chronic degeneration, sickening (– sickness is, broadly speaking, already a phenomenon consequent upon decay, *not* the cause of it), then he can be accorded little value, and elementary fairness demands that he *take away* as little as possible from the well-constituted. He is no better than a parasite on them . . .[51]

According to Nietzsche, historical ages, aesthetics, and moralities can also be described as belonging to either ascending life or declining life. Historically, he explained that "every age also possesses a measure for what virtues are permitted and forbidden to it." [52]

> Either it has the virtues of *ascending* life: then it will resist from the profoundest depths the virtues of declining life. Or the age itself represents declining life: then it also requires the virtues of decline, then it hates everything that justifies itself solely out of abundance, out of the overflowing riches of strength.[53]

Because aesthetics is "tied indissolubly to these biological presuppositions," there is also "an aesthetics of *decadence*" and "a *classical* aesthetics," the former belonging to declining life and the latter to ascending life.[54]

In "the narrower sphere of so-called moral values," master morality is an expression of ascending life, and the slave morality of Christianity is an expression of declining life. Master morality is "the sign language of what has turned out well, of *ascending* life, of the will to power as the principle of life." Master morality affirms life instinctively. It "gives to things out of its own abundance – it transfigures, it beautifies the world and *makes it more rational*."[55]

Master morality "is rooted in a triumphant Yes said to *oneself* – it is self-affirmation, self-glorification of life."[56] As practitioners of master morality, "pagans are all who say Yes to life, to whom 'God' is the word for the great Yes to all things."[57] The "prerequisites of *ascending* life" in the concept of god include the "strong, brave, masterful, [and] proud."[58] The "*ascending* movement of life" is represented by "well-constitutedness, power, beauty, self-affirmation on earth," all of which can be summarized as "*life-affirmation*."[59] The will to power is "the strongest, most life-affirming drive."[60]

As the fundamental phenomenon of life, the concept of the will to power provided the basis of Nietzsche's definition of good and bad in a new master morality.

> What is good? – All that heightens the feeling of power, the will to power, power itself in man.
> What is bad? – All that proceeds from weakness.
> What is happiness? – The feeling that power *increases* – that a resistance is overcome.
> *Not* contentment, but more power; *not* peace at all, but war; *not* virtue, but proficiency (virtue in the Renaissance style, *virtù*, virtue free of moralic acid).[61]

Later in the same book, Nietzsche expanded his definition of bad to include "everything that proceeds from weakness, from envy, from *revengefulness*."[62]

67

In this way, Nietzsche solved "the *problem of value*, the determination of the *order of rank among values*," that he set forth in an earlier book as "the future task of the philosophers." He placed the will to power at the top of his new order of rank among values because it would produce "a stronger type."[63] The will to power and its manifestations – power itself in its many forms, ascending life, and life affirmation – form the basis of Nietzsche's standard of value in his new master morality. To create the values of a new morality based on this new standard, however, a philosopher must be "beyond good and evil."

C. Beyond Good and Evil

As an immoralist, Nietzsche was beyond good and evil. Not only did he negate Christian morality, but he negated "the good" as well because "the good" are unable to create. In order to create new values, a creator must annihilate old values, but for that reason, the creator is "evil" according to the old values and thus no longer "the good." Nevertheless, the creator of new values is "good" according to his new valuation and thus beyond the good and evil of the old valuation. Being "beyond good and evil," therefore, is the precondition to the creation of the values of a new master morality.

Nietzsche chose Zarathustra as his mouthpiece in *Zarathustra* because the historical Zarathustra was the first to create a slave morality based on the dichotomy of good and evil (which was later adopted by Judaism, Christianity, and Islam) and thus Nietzsche's Zarathustra had to be the first to recognize it.

> I have not been asked, as I should have been asked, what the name of Zarathustra means in my mouth, the mouth of the first immoralist: for what constitutes the tremendous historical uniqueness of that Persian is just the opposite of this. Zarathustra was the first to consider the fight of good and evil the very wheel in the machinery of things: the transposition of morality into the metaphysical realm, as a force, cause, and end in itself, is *his* work. But this question itself is at bottom its own answer. Zarathustra created this most calamitous error, morality; consequently, he must also be the first to recognize it. [. . .] The self-overcoming of morality, out of truth-

fulness; the self-overcoming of the moralist, into his opposite – into me – that is what the name of Zarathustra means in my mouth.[64]

The opposite of a moralist is an immoralist. That is exactly what Nietzsche called himself. "I am the first immoralist: that makes me the annihilator *par excellence*."[65]

The term immoralist involves "two negations. For one, I negate a type of man that has so far been considered supreme: the good, the benevolent, the beneficent. And then I negate a type of morality that has become prevalent and predominant as morality itself – the morality of decadence or, more concretely, *Christian* morality."[66] On the second negation, Nietzsche added, "Nobody yet has felt *Christian* morality to be *beneath* him: that requires a height, a view of distances, a hitherto altogether unheard-of psychological depth and profundity."[67]

In regard to this second negation, "beyond good and evil" means feeling that Christian morality is beneath one. "We should be *able* also to stand *above* morality."[68] This feeling of standing above Christian morality – the feeling that morality is beneath one – is only possible when one realizes that there are no Christian moral facts.

> One knows my demand of philosophers that they place themselves *beyond* good and evil – that they have the illusion of moral judgment *beneath* them. This demand follows from an insight first formulated by me: *that there are no moral facts whatever*. Moral judgment has this in common with religious judgment that it believes in realities which do not exist. Morality is only an interpretation of certain phenomena, more precisely a *mis*interpretation.[69]

More succinctly, Nietzsche elsewhere wrote, "There are no moral phenomena at all, but only a moral interpretation of phenomena."[70]

In recognizing that there are no Christian moral facts and that "life *is* something essentially amoral,"[71] one feels that Christian morality is beneath one and thus places oneself beyond good and evil. To express it another way, beyond good and evil means no longer thinking "under the spell and delusion of morality."[72] Only in this way may one create a new master morality based on the dichotomy of good and bad.

The creation of a new morality also requires the immoralist's first negation: the negation of "the good, the benevolent, the beneficent." Nietzsche objected to Christianity's "demand that all should become 'good human beings,' herd animals, blue-eyed, benevolent, 'beautiful souls,'" because it "would deprive existence of its *great* character and would castrate men and reduce them to the level of desiccated Chinese stagnation."[73]

In explaining the need for "a *critique* of [Christian] moral values," Nietzsche raised the possibility that instead of "the good man" having greater value than "the evil man [. . .] in the sense of furthering the advancement and prosperity of man in general (the future of man included)," perhaps the reverse were true.[74]

> What if a symptom of regression were inherent in the "good," [. . .] through which the present was possibly living *at the expense of the future*? [. . .] So that precisely morality would be to blame if the *highest power and splendor* actually possible to the type man was never in fact attained? So that precisely morality was the danger of dangers?[75]

Additionally, Nietzsche rejected the simplistic division of humanity into "useful and harmful, good and evil men" because even "the most harmful man may really be the most useful when it comes to the preservation of the species."[76] In a section entitled "What preserves the species," Nietzsche wrote,

> The strongest and most evil spirits have so far done the most to advance humanity: again and again they relumed the passions that were going to sleep – all ordered society puts the passions to sleep – and they reawakened again and again the sense of comparison, of contradiction, of the pleasure in what is new, daring, untried; they compelled men to pit opinion against opinion, model against model. Usually by force of arms, by toppling boundary markers, by violating pieties – but also by means of new religions and moralities. In every

teacher and preacher of what is *new* we encounter the same "wickedness" that makes conquerors notorious, even if its expression is subtler and it does not immediately set the muscles in motion, and therefore also does not make one that notorious. What is new, however, is always *evil*, being that which wants to conquer and overthrow the old boundary markers and the old pieties; and only what is old is good. The good men are in all ages those who dig the old thoughts, digging deep and getting them to bear fruit – the farmers of the spirit. But eventually all land is exploited, and the ploughshare of evil must come again and again.[77]

Furthermore, conventional wisdom "holds that what is called good preserves the species, while what is called evil harms the species. In truth, however, the evil instincts are expedient, species-preserving, and indispensable to as high a degree as the good ones; their function is merely different."[78]

Throughout *Zarathustra*, "the good and the just," also called "the last men" and the "beginning of the end" as well as the "believers in the true faith,"[79] are the same as "the farmers of the spirit"[80] just quoted above. Collectively, they are the "good" and, as such, are the most harmful type of man. Nietzsche noted that "Zarathustra calls the good, now 'the last men,' now the 'beginning of the end'; above all, he considers them the most harmful type of man because they prevail at the expense of *truth* and at the expense of the *future*."[81] Quoting *Zarathustra*, Nietzsche explained that the "good are unable to *create*; they are always the beginning of the end; they crucify him who writes new values on new tablets; they sacrifice the future to *themselves* – they sacrifice all man's future."[82]

The "good" sacrifice humanity's future because they are unable to create and persecute those who do. After the people's rejection of his gift, Zarathustra decides to lure companions away from the herd and its shepherds. The shepherds, who are "the good and the just" and "the believers in the true faith," hate most the "man who breaks their tables of values, the breaker, the lawbreaker; yet he is the creator." The creators are "those who write new values on new tablets." Nevertheless, they will be called "destroyers" and "despisers of good and evil" by "the good and the just."[83]

In *Ecce Homo*, Nietzsche explained that, because the good are unable to create, Zarathustra, as "the first psychologist of the good," is "a friend of the evil."[84] Zarathustra's says

> that it was his insight precisely into the good, the "best," that made him shudder at man in general; that it was from *this* aversion that he grew wings "to soar off into distant futures"; he does not conceal the fact that *his* type of man, a relatively superhuman [*übermenschlicher*] type, is superhuman [*übermenschlich*] precisely in its relation to the *good* – that the good and the just would call his overman [*Übermensch*] *devil.*[85]

Only one considered as the "devil" or "evil" by the "good" is truly creative. Zarathustra teaches that "what is good and evil *no one knows yet*, unless it be he who creates. He, however, creates man's goal and gives the earth its meaning and its future. That anything at all is good and evil – that is his creation."[86] With their will to power, men "gave themselves all their good and evil." In other words, values are man-made. They are created by creators and a change of creators means a change of values. "Change of values – that is a change of creators. Whoever must be a creator always annihilates."[87]

Zarathustra also teaches that the concepts of good and evil are transitory: "good and evil that are not transitory, do not exist." Values are continually overcome. A creator must annihilate the old values of a previous creator before replacing them with his own new values. "And whoever must be a creator in good and evil, verily, he must first be an annihilator and break values. Thus the highest evil belongs to the highest goodness: but this is creative."[88] The annihilation of the old morality sets the conditions for the creation of a new morality.

Speaking to his animals immediately after his redemption, Zarathustra says that "only this have I learned so far, that man needs what is most evil in him for what is best in him – that whatever is most evil is his best power and the hardest stone for the highest creator; and that man must become better and more evil." His disgust with man was "that his greatest evil is so very small!"[89] In his speech on the higher man, Zarathustra says, "'Man is evil' – thus said all the wisest to comfort me. Alas, if only it were still true today! For evil is man's best strength. 'Man must become better and more evil' – thus *I* teach. The greatest evil is necessary for the overman's best."[90]

Consistent with Zarathustra's (and Nietzsche's) admonition that humanity must become more "evil" to be creative is his creation of a new value – become hard! "For creators are hard."[91] The "imperative" to "become hard!" reflects "the most fundamental certainty *that all creators are hard.*"[92]

Zarathustra places over his brothers this new tablet – become hard! – after placing another new tablet over them called a "new nobility."[93] Because "the good and the just" will be the enemy of Zarathustra's new value of a new nobility, the additional value of hardness is necessary in order to prevail in the struggle against "the good and the just" for the establishment of this new nobility.

D. New Nobility

According to Nietzsche, the "greatest of all tasks" is "the higher breeding of humanity"[94] and the goal of this task is the "enhancement" (*die Erhöhung*) of the type "man."[95] Because he thought that this enhancement could only be accomplished in an aristocratic society, Nietzsche advocated the establishment of a "new nobility" (*einer neue Adel*) that would restore the natural order of an aristocratic society and that would, within this society, tackle the task of the higher breeding of humanity in order to enhance the type "man." The higher breeding of humanity, which will be discussed in the next section, includes the "breeding" of a new nobility.

In his final weighing of the world before his redemption, Zarathustra places a new tablet over his "brothers" called a "new nobility." A new nobility is "needed to be the adversary of all rabble and of all that is despotic and to write anew upon new tablets the word 'noble.' For many who are noble are needed, and noble men of many kinds, that there may be a nobility."[96] Zarathustra "dedicates" and "directs" his brothers to a new nobility. The brothers "shall become procreators [*Zeuger*] and cultivators [*Züchter*] and sowers of the future [*Sämänner der Zukunft*]."[97] The new nobility

73

should not look backward but ahead! Exiles shall you be from all father- and forefather-lands! Your *children's land* shall you love: this love shall be your new nobility – the undiscovered land in the most distant sea. For that I bid your sails search and search.

In your children you shall make up for being the children of your fathers: thus shall you redeem all that is past. This new tablet I place over you.[98]

Nietzsche continued his advocacy for the establishment of a new nobility that would create new values and higher types in his next book, *Beyond Good and Evil*, which he called a *"critique of modernity."* It points "to a contrary type that is as little modern as possible – a noble, Yes-saying type" – and in this sense, is a "school for the *gentilhomme* ["nobleman"], taking this concept in a more spiritual and radical sense than has ever been done."[99]

In the book's last chapter entitled "What is Noble," Nietzsche examined the characteristics of both the aristocratic society and the noble individual.[100] Although he attempted "to write anew upon new tablets the word 'noble,'"[101] he left many tablets blank. Nevertheless, he completed the tablet that declared that human enhancement requires an aristocratic society with a good and healthy nobility that has, as its purpose, this very goal of human enhancement.

In the first section of the last chapter of *Beyond Good and Evil*, Nietzsche asserted that the "enhancement of the type 'man'" (*die Erhöhung des Typus "Mensch"*) is only possible in an aristocratic society – a society organized in a hierarchical social structure, that is, with an "order of rank" and with some form of slavery, "for every strengthening and enhancement of the human type also involves a new kind of enslavement."[102]

Every enhancement of the type "man" has so far been the work of an aristocratic society – and it will be so again and again – a society that believes in the long ladder of an order of rank and differences in value between man and man, and that needs slavery in some sense or other. Without that *pathos of distance* which grows out of the ingrained difference between strata – when the ruling caste constantly looks afar and looks down upon subjects and instruments and just as constantly practices obedience and command, keeping down and keeping at a distance – that other, more mysterious pathos could not have grown up either – the craving for an ever new widening of distances within the soul itself, the development of ever higher, rarer, more remote, further-stretching, more comprehensive states – in brief, simply the enhancement of the type "man," the continual "self-overcoming of man," to use a moral formula in a supra-moral sense.[103]

Without yielding to "humanitarian illusions" because the "truth is hard," Nietzsche explained "the origins of an aristocratic society (and thus of the pre-supposition of this enhancement of the type 'man')" and "how every higher culture on earth so far has *begun*."[104]

Human beings whose nature was still natural, barbarians in every terrible sense of the word, men of prey who were still in possession of unbroken strength of will and lust for power, hurled themselves upon weaker, more civilized, more peaceful races, perhaps traders or cattle raisers, or upon mellow old cultures whose last vitality was even then flaring up in splendid fireworks of spirit and corruption. In the beginning, the noble caste was always the barbarian caste: their predominance did not lie mainly in physical strength but in strength of the soul – they were more *whole* human beings (which also means, at every level, "more whole beasts").[105]

In *The Anti-Christ*, Nietzsche explained that every healthy society established in this way naturally divides itself into three classes corresponding to the three types of humanity. Nature "separates from one another the predominately spiritual type, the predominately muscular and temperamental type, and the third type distinguished neither in the one nor the other, the mediocre type – the last as the great majority, the first as the elite." He used the Law of Manu as an example because the *"order of castes* [in Law of Manu], the supreme, the dominating law, is only the sanctioning of a *natural order.*"[106]

75

The "noble caste" or "the elite" are the "highest caste," "*the very few*," and the "perfect caste," consisting of the "most spiritual human beings, as the *strongest*," who can affirm that the "*world is perfect*." They have the "instinct of the most spiritual, the affirmative instinct." They are the "most venerable kind of human being" and "rule not because they want to but because they *are*; they are not free to be second in rank."[107] As Zarathustra says, "the best should rule, the best also want to rule. And where the doctrine is different, there the best is *lacking*."[108]

The second in rank are

> the guardians of the law, the keepers of order and security; the noble warriors; above all the *king* as the highest formula of warrior, judge and upholder of the law. The second in rank are the executives of the most spiritual order, the closest to them who relieve them of everything *coarse* in the work of ruling – their following, their right hand, their best pupils.[109]

The difference between the first and second in rank is reflected in the difference between the institutions of a church and a state.

> A church is above all a structure for ruling that secures the highest rank for the *more spiritual* human beings and that *believes* in the power of spirituality to the extent of forbidding itself the use of all the cruder instruments of force; and on this score alone the church is under all circumstances a *nobler* institution than the state.[110]

The broad base of this cultural pyramid is "a strongly and soundly consolidated mediocrity. The crafts, trade, agriculture, *science*, the greater part of art, in a word the entire compass of *professional* activity, are in no way compatible with anything other than mediocrity in ability and desires." There should be no objection in mediocrity as such because it is "the *prime* requirement for the existence of exceptions: a high culture is conditional upon it."[111]

Not only is high culture dependent upon this natural order of society, such an order is also necessary for the creation of "higher types."

The order of castes, *order of rank*, only formulates the supreme law of life itself; the separation of the three types is necessary for the preservation of society, for making possible higher and higher types – *inequality* of rights is the condition for the existence of rights at all. – A right is a privilege. The privilege of each is determined by the nature of his being.[112]

As the product of the enhancement of the type "man," these "higher types" can only come into existence when the nobility or aristocracy is "good and healthy."

The essential characteristic of a good and healthy aristocracy, however, is that it experiences itself *not* as a function (whether of the monarchy or the commonwealth) but as their *meaning* and highest justification – that it therefore accepts with a good conscience the sacrifice of untold human beings who, *for its sake*, must be reduced and lowered to incomplete human beings, to slaves, to instruments. Their fundamental faith simply has to be that society must *not* exist for society's sake but only as the foundation and scaffolding on which a choice type of being is able to raise itself to its higher task and to a higher state of *being* [. . .][113]

This "higher task" is the higher breeding of humanity and its goal is this "higher state of *being*," that is, the enhancement of the type "man" or, as quoted earlier, "the development of ever higher, rarer, more remote, further-stretching, more comprehensive states."[114]

E. Higher Breeding of Humanity

As the greatest of all tasks, the "higher breeding of humanity" (*die Höherzüchtung der Menschheit*)[115] envisaged by Nietzsche is a conscious project for the enhancement of the type "man" through not only the "breeding" (*Züchtung*) of higher types, but also the breeding of a new nobility and a new European race. Although using the term *Züchtung*, which has a primarily biological denotation, Nietzsche gave it a dual biological-cultural meaning.

As early as his *Untimely Meditations* (1873-1876), Nietzsche called for "the production of the great man,"[116] that is, a higher human type. He wrote that "the *goal of humanity* cannot lie in its end but only *in its highest exemplars*."[117] The highest exemplars are "those true *men, those who are no longer animal, the philosophers, artists and saints*." Therefore, it is "the fundamental idea of *culture*, insofar as it sets for each one of us but one task: *to promote the production of the philosopher, the artist and the saint within us and without us and thereby to work at the perfecting of nature*."[118]

For Nietzsche in this early period, the philosophers, artists, and saints were the only true human beings and the sole representatives of genius and, therefore, their production or procreation was the goal of culture. The "procreation of genius [. . .] is the goal of all culture."[119] "Mankind must work continually at the production of individual great men – that and nothing else is its task." The "goal of culture is to promote the production of true *human beings* and nothing else" and the "supreme goal" of culture is "the production of the genius."[120]

Foreshadowing his later concept of "the rare cases of great power of soul and body, man's *lucky hits*,"[121] Nietzsche also wrote in his untimely meditations,

> We ought really to have no difficulty in seeing that, when a species has arrived at its limits and is about to go over into a higher species, the goal of its evolution lies, not in the mass of its exemplars and their wellbeing, let alone in those exemplars who happen to come last in point of time, but rather in those apparently scattered and chance existences which favorable conditions have here and there produced; and it ought to be just as easy to understand the demand that, because it can arrive at a conscious awareness of its goal, mankind ought to seek out and create the favorable conditions under which those great redemptive men can come into existence.[122]

Although Nietzsche later changed his opinion about the possibility of humanity going over into a higher species,[123] he continued to recognize that humanity could consciously create its own evolutionary goal and breed a higher type – "those great redemptive men."[124] In another early book, Nietzsche wrote that

> men are capable of *consciously* resolving to evolve themselves to a new culture, whereas formerly they did so unconsciously and fortuitously: they can now create better conditions for the propagation of men and for their nutrition, education and instruction, manage the earth as a whole economically, balance and employ the powers of men in general.[125]

In his next book, Nietzsche wrote, while discussing biological evolution, that because mankind does not possess "a universally recognized *goal*," it is not "possible to propose 'thus and thus is the *right* course of action.'" Therefore, it is "irrational and trivial to impose the demands of morality upon mankind." We could, however, "*recommend* a goal to mankind," a goal "which *lies in our own discretion*" and if "the recommendation appealed to mankind, it could in pursuit of it also *impose* upon itself a moral law."[126]

Nietzsche was more direct about describing this conscious activity in his later notes. "What has been achieved here and there partly by hardship, partly by chance, the conditions for a *stronger species* to emerge, we can now understand and deliberately *will*: we can create the conditions under which such a heightening is possible."[127] This creation is possible because of the nature of man. "In man *creature* and *creator* are united: in man there is material, fragment, excess, clay, dirt, nonsense, chaos; but in man there is also creator, form-giver, hammer hardness, spectator divinity, and seventh day."[128]

In his works after *Zarathustra*, Nietzsche used the term *Züchtung* to describe his method of human enhancement. Although *Züchtung* means "breeding,"[129] as in the breeding of domestic animals, Nietzsche used it to describe both the biological and cultural aspects of his new method.[130] For example, using the term in its biological aspect, Nietzsche looked

> at an aristocratic commonwealth – say, an ancient Greek *polis* ["city-state"], or Venice – as an arrangement, whether voluntary or involuntary, for *breeding* [*Züchtung*]: human beings are

together there who are dependent on themselves and want their species to prevail, most often because they *have to* prevail or run the terrible risk of being exterminated.[131]

Then using the term in its cultural aspect with regard to the cultivation of virtues, Nietzsche continued in the same section:

Manifold experience teaches them to which qualities above all they owe the fact that, despite all gods and men, they are still there, that they have always triumphed: these qualities they call virtues, these virtues alone they cultivate [*züchten*]. They do this with hardness, indeed they want hardness; every aristocratic morality is intolerant – in the education of youth, in their arrangements for women, in their marriage customs, in the relations of old and young, in their penal laws (which take into account deviants only) – they consider intolerance itself a virtue, calling it "justice."[132]

This dual meaning and use of *Züchtung* and *züchten* reflects Nietzsche's Lamarckism. He accepted the Lamarckian idea of the "inheritance of acquired traits."[133] Blurring or ignoring the difference between biological and cultural inheritance,[134] Nietzsche believed that changes in traits acquired through upbringing, training, education, and other means can become inheritable.[135] "Breeding," therefore, meant for Nietzsche both biological methods (e.g., direct control of reproduction) and cultural methods (e.g., social techniques to change habits and values). Even so, he called his new project "breeding" in order to stress its biological aspect.[136]

Nietzsche still recognized the importance of upbringing, training, education, and other means of changing habits and values that may not become inheritable. This recognition was expressed in his frequent pairing of *Züchtung* with *Erziehung* ("upbringing" or "education").[137] For example, in *Beyond Good and Evil,* we find both "*Züchtungs- und Erziehungswerke*" ("project of breeding and education")[138] and "*Züchtungs- und Erziehungsmittel*" ("means of breeding and education").[139] He also paired "*Zucht und Züchtung*" ("discipline and breeding").[140]

In his books written in 1888, Nietzsche became less discreet in his language about "breeding" human beings. In *The Anti-Christ* – his "most independent"[141] book — Nietzsche raised the problem of

> not what ought to succeed mankind in the sequence of species (– the human being is an *end* –): but what type of human being one ought to *breed* [*züchten*], ought to *will*, as more valuable, more worthy of life, more certain of the future.
>
> This more valuable type has existed often enough already: but as a lucky accident, as an exception, never as *willed*.[142]

He explained further that

> there are cases of individual success constantly appearing in the most various parts of the earth and from the most various cultures in which a *higher type* does manifest itself: something which in relation to collective mankind is a sort of superman [*Übermensch*].[143] Such chance occurrences of great success have always been possible and perhaps always will be possible. And even entire races, tribes, nations can under certain circumstances represent such a *lucky hit*.[144]

At the same time, this more valuable or higher type has been the most feared "and out of fear the reverse type has been willed, bred, *achieved*: the domestic animal, the herd animal, the sick animal man – the Christian . . ."[145] Furthermore, Christianity "has waged a *war to the death* against this *higher* type of man, it has excommunicated all the fundamental instincts of this type, it has distilled evil, the *Evil One*, out of these instincts – the strong human being as the type of reprehensibility, as the 'outcast.'"[146]

Instead of relying on such "lucky hits" and to better defend against this Christian war on the higher type, Nietzsche insisted that the higher type of man must be consciously created, especially since "progress" does not necessarily mean an enhancement of the type "man."

Mankind does *not* represent a development of the better or the stronger or the higher in the way that is believed today. "Progress" is merely a modern idea, that is to say a false idea. The European of today is of far less value than the European of the Renaissance; onward development is not by *any* means, by any necessity the same thing as elevation, advance, strengthening.[147]

Although he rejected the modern idea of progress, Nietzsche accepted Darwin's theory of the origin of species by natural selection. "We no longer trace the origin of man in the 'spirit,' in the 'divinity,' we have placed him back among the animals."[148] He also agreed with the idea that humanity is not "the great secret objective of animal evolution. Man is absolutely not the crown of creation: every creature stands beside him at the same stage of perfection."[149] Nietzsche did not consider humanity "a goal but only a way, an episode, a bridge, a great promise."[150] Humanity "is the *as yet undetermined animal.*"[151]

Nevertheless, Nietzsche did not think that natural selection always results in the survival of the "lucky hits," the higher type of man.

Supposing, however, that this struggle exists – and it does indeed occur – its outcome is the reverse of that desired by the school of Darwin, of that which one *ought* perhaps to desire with them: namely, the defeat of the stronger, the more privileged, the fortunate exceptions. Species do *not* grow more perfect: the weaker dominate the strong again and again – the reason being they are the great majority, and they are also *cleverer.*[152]

In his notes of 1888, Nietzsche repeated his disagreement with the Darwinian school in this respect.

What surprises me most when surveying the great destinies of man is always seeing before me the opposite of what Darwin and his school see or *want to* see today: selection in favor of the stronger, in favor of those who have come off better, the progress of the species. The very opposite is quite palpably the case: the elimination of the strokes of luck, the use-lessness of the better-constituted types, the inevitable domination achieved by the average, even *below-average* types.[153]

For that reason, Nietzsche's higher breeding of humanity is a *conscious* project for the enhancement of the type "man" through the breeding of higher human types.[154] Although his primary goal is the creation of higher types, the project also necessarily includes the breeding of a new nobility and a new European race because the nobility and the race are the means to the end of higher types.[155] The breeding of higher types can only occur within an aristocratic society that has a "good and healthy"[156] nobility, as noted earlier,[157] and that is composed of a new European mixed race that has become "pure,"[158] as we shall see.

The conscious action that Nietzsche advocated for the higher breeding of humanity can be divided into two categories. Although he did not use these terms, these categories can be called positive and negative eugenics.[159] The methods of positive eugenics are designed to encourage the valuable to reproduce more, and the methods of negative eugenics are designed to discourage or prevent the harmful or unworthy from reproducing.[160]

1. Positive Eugenics

The primary method of positive eugenics advocated by Nietzsche was the control of marriage and thus of reproduction. This particular method not only applies to the breeding of higher types, it also applies to the breeding of a new nobility and a new race.[161] Nietzsche, however, rarely used the term *Züchtung* solely in its biological aspect. Therefore, when Nietzsche wrote about the breeding of higher types, of a new nobility or caste to rule Europe, and of a new European race, it is important to remember the dual biological-cultural meaning of *Züchtung* and that the "breeding" of higher types, a caste, or race also includes the social techniques to change habits and values.

In a few places in his early books, Nietzsche revealed his eugenic view of marriage. For example, he wanted "a good physician" to act "as promoter and preventer of marriages" for "the production of a spiritual-physical aristocracy."[162] Reflecting his Lamarckism, he also

83

wrote, "If we prevented the discontented, atrabilious and sullen from propagating themselves we could magically transform the earth into a garden of happiness."[163] In his next book, Nietzsche complained of "chance in marriage" because it "makes a grand rational progress of mankind impossible" and prevents the individual from thinking "that through procreation he could prepare the way for an even more victorious life."[164]

In *Zarathustra*, Nietzsche provided his most familiar eugenic statement on marriage and its purpose. In his speech on child and marriage, Zarathustra teaches his concept of marriage. For those worthy of reproducing, the purpose of marriage is to produce something higher, to create a creator, and to create the one that is more than those who create it.

> You shall build over and beyond yourself, but first you must be built yourself, perpendicular in body and soul. You shall not only reproduce yourself, but produce something higher. May the garden of marriage help you in that!
>
> You shall create a higher body, a first movement, a self-propelled wheel – you shall create a creator.
>
> Marriage: thus I name the will of two to create the one that is more than those who created it. Reverence for each other, as for those willing with such a will, is what I name marriage. Let this be the meaning and truth of your marriage.[165]

In his final word on the subject, Zarathustra counsels his brothers on marriage. "Not merely to reproduce, but to produce something *higher* – toward that, my brothers, the garden of marriage should help you." He rhetorically adds, "what would my love for the overman and for all who shall yet come amount to if I counseled and spoke differently?"[166] This rhetorical question suggests that the production of something higher, such as the Overman, includes the cultural method of breeding, rather than only the biological act of procreation because, as discussed earlier,[167] the Overman is not a product of biological evolution.

This dual aspect of Nietzsche' project of human enhancement is also reflected in his important discussion of the "improvers" of humanity.[168] He made a distinction between two ways of "improving" humanity – "taming" (*Zähmung*) and "breeding" (*Züchtung*) – but only approved of breeding. "In all ages one has wanted to 'improve' men: this above all is what morality has meant. [. . .] Both the *taming* [*Zähmung*] of the beast man and the *breeding* [*Züchtung*] of a certain species of man has been called 'improvement.'"[169] These terms, however, are commonly confused.

In his notes of 1888, Nietzsche complained "that there is no worse confusion than the confusion of breeding [*Züchtung*] with taming [*Zähmung*]: which is what has been done." As he understood it, *Züchtung* "is a means of storing up the tremendous forces of mankind so that the generations can build upon the work of their forefathers – not only outwardly, but inwardly, organically growing out of them and becoming something stronger" and "the goal of breeding [*Züchtung*], even in the case of a single individual, can only be the *stronger* man (– the man without breeding is weak, extravagant, unstable –)."[170] This understanding of breeding is consistent with Nietzsche's dual meaning and use of the term *Züchtung* in his published works.

We have already noted Christian morality as an example of "the *taming* of the beast man."[171] In contrast to Christianity, Nietzsche described the ancient Indian "Law of Manu," that is, Aryan morality sanctioned into religion, as the "most grandiose example" of "the *breeding* [*Züchtung*] of a definite race and species."[172] In fact,

> the proposed task is to breed no fewer than four races simultaneously: a priestly, a warrior, and a trading and farming race, and finally a menial race, the Sudras. Here we are manifestly no longer among animal-tamers: a species of human being a hundred times more gentle and rational is presupposed even to conceive the plan of such a breeding.[173]

Nietzsche called the Law of Manu a "healthier, higher, *wider* world" when compared with "the Christian sick-house and dungeon atmosphere." "How paltry the 'New Testament' is compared with Manu, how ill it smells!" Yet, he then described how "*dreadful*" Manu treated "the hotchpotch human being, the Chandala,"[174] the name of the "untouchables" excluded from the Indian caste system. Although he seemingly disapproved of this particular treatment of the Chandala,[175] Nietzsche generally praised the Law of Manu. In his next book, he called the book of Manu "an incomparably spiritual and superior work, so much as to *name* which in the same breath as the Bible would be a sin against the *spirit*."[176]

As noted earlier,[177] Nietzsche used the Law of Manu as an example of the moral sanctioning of a natural order. In the restoration of such a natural order by a new nobility, he found the solution to the "European problem." As Nietzsche understood it, the "European problem" was the lack of political unity in Europe caused by the divisive effects of nationalism.[178] He called nationalism "this most *anti-cultural* sickness and unreason there is [. . .] this *névrose nationale* ["national neurosis"] with which Europe is sick, this perpetuation of European particularism, of *petty* politics."[179] Political disunity prevented "the good Europeans" from coming "into possession of their great task: the direction and supervision of the total culture of the earth."[180]

Although calling it the problem itself, Nietzsche actually identified the solution to the European problem. Touching on what is "*serious*" to him in *Beyond Good and Evil*, he identified the solution to be "the cultivation [*Züchtung*] of a new caste that will rule Europe."[181] As a "thinker who has the development of Europe on his conscience,"[182] Nietzsche thought that the breeding of a new nobility or "caste" (*die Kaste*) was the solution to the problem of European political disunity. A new ruling caste could overcome "the insanity of nationality" because he saw "the most unequivocal portents [. . .] that *Europe wants to become one*."[183]

One way Europe could become one is by unifying against a common enemy. Looking at the political situation in Europe, Nietzsche observed that Russia was Europe's "greatest danger." To decrease the menace of Russia, it would take "internal upheavals" and "above all the introduction of the parliamentary nonsense"[184] in Russia. He, however, would prefer

an increase in the menace of Russia that Europe would have to resolve to become menacing, too, namely, *to acquire one will* by means of a new caste that would rule Europe, a long, terrible will of its own that would be able to cast its goals millennia hence – so the long-drawn-out comedy of its many splinter states as well as its dynastic and democratic splinter wills would come to an end. The time for petty politics is over: the very next century will bring the fight for the dominion of the earth – the *compulsion* to large-scale politics.[185]

In addition to a new caste or nobility that would unify and rule Europe, Nietzsche advocated the breeding of a new European race to facilitate the unification of Europe and to "achieve a pure European race and culture."[186] Complaining that we live in an "age of disintegration that mixes races indiscriminately,"[187] Nietzsche expressed definite views about the possibility and desirability of breeding a new European race.

In one of his early books, Nietzsche predicted a "weakening and finally an abolition of nations, at least the European: so that as a consequence of continual crossing a mixed race, that of European man, must come into being out of them." Yet, "the separation of nations through the production of *national* hostilities" by "certain princely dynasties" and "certain classes of business and society," producing an "artificial nationalism," is working against this inevitable goal. When one has recognized this fact, Nietzsche declared that "one should not be afraid to proclaim oneself simply a *good European* and actively to work for the amalgamation of nations."[188]

Later, Nietzsche wrote that because of Europe's democratic movement, "a tremendous *physiological* process is taking place and gaining momentum" in which the "Europeans are becoming more similar to each other [. . .] Thus an essentially supra-national and nomadic type of man is gradually coming up, a type that possesses, physiologically speaking, a maximum of the art and power of adaptation as its typical distinction." Despite being "retarded by great relapses" such as "the still raging storm and stress of 'national feeling,'" he saw the "tempo of this process of the '*evolving European*'" as perhaps gaining in vehemence and profundity and growing on account of these relapses.[189]

Nietzsche included the Jews in this European "amalgamation of nations" and this process of the "evolving European." "As soon as it is no longer a question of the conserving of nations but of the production of the strongest possible European mixed race, the Jew will be just as usable and desirable as an ingredient of it as any other national residue."[190] In a later book, however, he modified his views as to the quality and quantity of Jews that should be included in this new European race. Nietzsche considered the Jews as "the strongest, toughest, and purest race now living in Europe," but, he observed, they want "to be absorbed and assimilated by Europe." He suggested that this Jewish impulse "be noted well and *accommodated*" but accommodated "with all caution, with selection; approximately as the English nobility does."[191] Moreover, he admitted that

> Germany has amply *enough* Jews, that the German stomach, the German blood has trouble (and will still have trouble for a long time) digesting even this quantum of "Jew" – as the Italians, French, and English have done, having a stronger digestive system – that is the clear testimony and language of a general instinct to which one must listen, in accordance with which one must act.[192]

Recognizing that what was normal is "crossed races," Nietzsche still hoped that "a pure European race and culture" could be achieved. He explained that there "are probably no pure races but only races that have become pure, even these being extremely rare" and that what "is normal is crossed races." Even so, "the Greeks offer us the model of a race and culture that has become pure" through "countless adaptations, absorptions and secretions." Like all pure races, the Greeks also became "*stronger* and *more beautiful*." He added at the end of the section that "hopefully we shall one day also achieve a pure European race and culture."[193]

Reflecting this hope and his bias toward which type of European he preferred, Nietzsche was concerned about the emergence or "counterattack" in his day of Europe's "pre-Aryan" people. In his etymological inquiry into the origin of noble morality in *Genealogy of Morals*, he suggested that the Latin word *malus* ("bad"), which he set beside the Greek word *melas* ("black, dark"), may designate the common man as the dark-skinned, above all as the black-haired man [. . .], as the pre-Aryan occupant of the soil of Italy who was distinguished most obviously from the blond, that is Aryan, conqueror race by his color; Gaelic, at any rate, offers us a precisely similar case – *fin* (for example in the name *Fin-Gal*), the distinguishing word for nobility, finally for the good, noble, pure, originally meant the blond-headed, in contradistinction to the dark, black-haired aboriginal inhabitants.[194]

Nietzsche continued by stating that the Celts "were definitely a blond race" and, therefore, were not the source of the "essentially dark-haired people" who were emerging throughout Europe. He was concerned that "the *pre-Aryan* people," this

suppressed race has gradually recovered the upper hand again, in coloring, shortness of skull, perhaps even in the intellectual and social instincts: who can say whether modern democracy, even more modern anarchism and especially that inclination for "*commune*," for the most primitive form of society, which is now shared by all the socialists of Europe, does not signify in the main a tremendous *counterattack* – and that the conqueror and *master race* [*die Eroberer- und Herren-Rasse*], the Aryan, is not succumbing physiologically, too?[195]

According to Nietzsche, not only do the pre-Aryan people pose a political and biological threat to the Aryan through its "*counterattack*," but the Aryan is becoming genetically devalued by succumbing physiologically, too. This latter consequence was largely caused by the dysgenic effects of Christianity.

2. Negative Eugenics

The primary method of negative eugenics advocated by Nietzsche was the prevention of the reproduction of those unworthy of doing so, by destruction if necessary. The creative task of the higher breeding of humanity includes destructive acts, such as "the relentless destruction of everything that was degenerating and parasitical."[196] For that

89

reason, Nietzsche criticized Christianity for preserving those who ought to perish. By saving the unworthy, Christianity subverts the principle of natural selection.[197]

Nietzsche considered the many as only a means to the enhancement of the few. "The magnitude of an 'advance' can even be measured by the mass of things that had to be sacrificed to it; mankind in the mass sacrificed to the prosperity of a single *stronger* species of man – that *would* be an advance."[198] He repeated this sentiment in his notes. "The basic phenomenon: countless individuals sacrificed for the sake of a few, to make them possible. – One must not let oneself be deceived; it is just the same with peoples and races: they constitute the 'body' for the production of isolated valuable individuals, who carry on the great process."[199] "Basic errors of biologists hitherto: it is not a question of the species but of more powerful individuals. (The many are only a means)."[200] "We must think of the masses as unsentimentally as we think of nature: they preserve the species."[201]

To achieve this "advance," Nietzsche proposed a new "*moral code for physicians*" in which a new responsibility is created for the physician "in all cases in which the highest interest of life, of *ascending* life, demands the most ruthless suppression and sequestration of degenerating life – for example in determining the right to reproduce, the right to be born, the right to live."[202] This proposal corrects the most common erroneous conclusion drawn by humanity: "a thing exists, therefore it has a right to. Here the conclusion is from the capacity to live to the fitness to live, from the fitness to live to the right to live."[203]

In a section that was originally intended to be included in *Twilight of the Idols* entitled "My Categorical Imperative" but withdrawn after he corrected the printer's proof, Nietzsche described society's duty to such degenerating life.

> After all, society has a *duty* here: few more pressing and fundamental demands can be made upon it. Society, as the great trustee of life, is responsible to life itself for every miscarried life – it also has to pay for such lives: consequently it ought to prevent them. In numerous cases, society ought to prevent procreation: to this end, it may hold in readiness, without regard to descent, rank, or spirit, the most rigorous means of

constraint, deprivation of freedom, in certain circumstances castration. –

The Biblical prohibition "thou shalt not kill!" is a piece of naiveté compared with the seriousness of the prohibition of life to decadents: "thou shalt not procreate!" – Life itself recognizes no solidarity, no "equal rights," between the healthy and the degenerate parts of an organism: one must excise the latter – or the whole will perish. – Sympathy for decadents, equal rights for the ill-constituted – that would be the profoundest immorality, that would be antinature itself as morality![204]

The "first principle" of Nietzsche's "philanthropy" is that the "weak and ill-constituted shall perish [. . .] And one shall help them to do so." Consistent with this principle, Nietzsche criticized Christianity for its dysgenic effects on humanity. "What is more harmful than any vice? – Active sympathy for the ill-constituted and weak – Christianity."[205] "Christianity has taken the side of everything weak, base, ill-constituted, it has made an ideal out of *opposition* to the preservative instincts of strong life."[206]

The Christian virtues of pity and selflessness subvert natural selection by preventing the weak and sick from being "selected out."[207]

Pity on the whole thwarts the law of evolution, which is the law of *selection*. It preserves what is ripe for destruction; it defends life's disinherited and condemned; through the abundance of the ill-constituted of all kinds which it *retains* in life it gives life itself a gloomy and questionable aspect.[208]

Of those who were already "sick, degenerating, infirm," or otherwise "did not turn out right," Christianity "preserved too much of *what ought to perish*." It sought "to preserve alive whatever can possibly be preserved" and agreed "with all those who suffer life like a sickness and would like to make sure that every other feeling about life should be considered false and should become impossible." This attitude was "among the chief causes that have kept the type 'man' on a lower rung." Christianity preserved "all that was sick and that suffered –

which means, in fact and in truth, to *worsen the European race.*" In order to do so, as already noted,[209] the church had to "stand all valuations *on their head.*" It had to "invert all love of the earthly and of dominion over the earth into hatred of the earth and the earthly."[210]

After a long list of attacks on Christianity at the end of *Ecce Homo,* Nietzsche concluded,

> Finally – this is what is most terrible of all – the concept of the *good* man signifies that one sides with all that is weak, sick, failure, suffering of itself – all that ought to perish: the principle of selection is crossed – an ideal is fabricated from the contradiction against the proud and well-turned-out human being who says Yes, who is sure of the future, who guarantees the future – and he is now called *evil.* – And all this was believed, *as morality!*[211]

In opposition to the order of rank and pathos of distance required of an aristocratic society (the precondition for the enhancement of the type "man"), Christianity has sowed the "poison of the doctrine '*equal rights for all*'" and "from the most secret recesses of base instincts, Christianity has waged a war to the death against every feeling of reverence and distance between man and man, against, that is, the *precondition* of every elevation, every increase in culture."[212] "'Equality' [. . .] belongs essentially to decline: the chasm between man and man, class and class, the multiplicity of types, the will to be oneself, to stand out – that which I call *pathos of distance* – characterizes every *strong* age."[213]

Christianity "has forged out of the *ressentiment* of the masses its *chief weapon* against *us,* against everything noble, joyful, high-spirited on earth, against our happiness on earth."[214] As a result,

> no one any longer possesses today the courage to claim special privileges or the right to rule, the courage to feel a sense of reverence towards himself and towards his equals – the courage for a *pathos of distance.* . . . Our politics is *morbid* from this lack of courage! – The aristocratic outlook has been undermined most deeply by the lie of equality of souls; and if the belief in the "prerogative of the majority" makes revolu-

tions and *will continue to make them* – it is Christianity, let there be no doubt about it, *Christian* value judgment which translates every revolution into mere blood and crime![215]

Nietzsche repeated similar ideas in his notebooks. He called the "equality of men" the "greatest of all lies."[216]

If one regards individuals as equal, one calls the species into question, one encourages a way of life that leads to the ruin of the species: Christianity is the counterprinciple to the principle of *selection*. [. . .] The species requires that the ill-constituted, weak, degenerate, perish: but it was precisely to them that Christianity turned as a conserving force.[217]

To prevent a further worsening of the European race by Christianity, Nietzsche wanted to reverse – through his revaluation of all values and the creation of a new philosophy of the future – the inversion of noble values that the Jews began and the Christians continued. As already discussed,[218] a key concept of his philosophy of the future is a new nobility. Critical to the establishment of this new nobility is the appearance of "philosophers of the future."

F. Philosophers of the Future

Nietzsche was the herald and precursor of future creators of new values that he called "philosophers of the future."[219] He was also the first of those he heralded. The tasks he assigned to these philosophers of the future are to complete the philosophy of the future, his new master morality that he had commenced, and to establish a new nobility that would tackle the task of the higher breeding of humanity.

Like Zarathustra who becomes the Overman that he at first heralded, Nietzsche is the first philosopher of the future.[220] Of these future philosophers, Nietzsche called himself one of "their heralds and precursors, we free spirits."[221] He had called his long-sought-after disciples or followers in many of his earlier books by the name of "free spirits," by which he meant "a spirit that has *become free*, that has again taken possession of itself."[222] Slightly modifying that expression, he called his philosophers of the future "free, *very* free spirits."[223]

These philosophers of the future will not only be "free, *very* free spirits [. . .] but something more, higher, greater, and thoroughly different that does not want to be misunderstood and mistaken for something else."[224] Nietzsche called the "falsely so-called 'free spirits'" of his time – "being eloquent and prolifically scribbling slaves of the democratic taste and its 'modern ideas'" – by the name of "*levelers*" who

> find in the forms of the old society as it has existed so far just about the cause of *all* human misery and failure – which is a way of standing truth happily upon her head! What they would like to strive for with all their powers is the universal green-pasture happiness of the herd, with security, lack of danger, comfort, and an easier life for everyone; the two songs and doctrines which they repeat most often are "equality of rights" and "sympathy for all that suffers" – and suffering itself they take for something that must be *abolished*.[225]

Nietzsche and other true "free spirits" were the opposites and antipodes of these levelers. He asserted that only the "discipline of suffering, of *great* suffering [. . .] has created all enhancements of man so far."[226]

> We opposite men, having opened our eyes and conscience to the question where and how the plant "man" has so far grown most vigorously to a height – we think that this has happened every time under the opposite conditions, that to this end the dangerousness of his situation must first grow to the point of enormity, his power of invention and simulation (his "spirit") had to develop under prolonged pressure and constraint into refinement and audacity, his life-will had to be enhanced into an unconditional power-will. We think that hardness, forcefulness, slavery, danger in the alley and the heart, life in hiding, stoicism, the art of experiment and devilry of every kind, that everything evil, terrible, tyrannical in man, everything in him that is kin to beasts of prey and serpents, serves the enhancement of the species "man" as much as its opposite does. Indeed, we do not even say

enough when we say only that much; and at any rate we are at this point, in what we say and keep silent about, at the *other* end from all modern ideology and herd desiderata – as their antipodes perhaps?[227]

At the end of the section, Nietzsche suggested that the philosophers of the future would share these views on the conditions required for the enhancement of humanity.

Nietzsche and other "opposite men" have a "different faith" than the faith of the levelers. Despairing of Christianity and the democratic movement as not only decadent but also corruptive of humanity, he rhetorically asked, "Where, then, must *we* then reach with our hopes?"

> Toward *new philosophers*; there is no choice; toward spirits strong and original enough to provide the stimuli for opposite valuations and to revalue and invert "eternal values"; toward forerunners, toward men of the future who in the present tie the knot and constraint that forces the will of millennia upon *new* tracks. To teach man the future of man as his *will*, as dependent on a human will, and to prepare great ventures and over-all attempts of discipline and cultivation [*Zucht und Züchtung*] by way of putting an end to that gruesome dominion of nonsense and accident that has so far been called "history" – the nonsense of the "greatest number" is merely its ultimate form: at some time new types of philosophers and commanders will be necessary for that, and whatever has existed on earth of concealed, terrible, and benevolent spirits, will look pale and dwarfed by comparison. It is the image of such leaders that *we* envisage: may I say this out loud, you free spirits?[228]

Failing the appearance of these "new types of philosophers and commanders" and "leaders" who will continue Nietzsche's revaluation of all values by completing the creation of a new master morality (i.e., "revalue and invert 'eternal values'") and who will establish a new nobility that would tackle the task of the higher breeding of humanity (i.e., "attempts of discipline and cultivation"), humanity will continue to degenerate under "the whole Christian-European morality" until the dominance of the "last man," who Nietzsche described in *Beyond Good and Evil* as the "degeneration and diminution of man into the perfect herd animal" and the "animalization of man into the dwarf animal of equal rights and claims."[229]

These new philosophers – philosophers of the future – will be "genuine" philosophers. Nietzsche distinguished between "philosophical laborers" and "genuine" philosophers. The education of a genuine philosopher may require the work of the "scientific laborers of philosophy," but the genuine philosopher's task "demands something different – it demands that he *create values*."[230] This is so because "it is the characteristic *right of masters* to create values."[231]

> *Genuine philosophers, however, are commanders and legislators*: they say, "*thus* it *shall* be!" They first determine the Whither and For What of man, and in so doing have at their disposal the preliminary labor of all philosophical laborers, all who have overcome the past. With a creative hand they reach for the future, and all that is and has been becomes a means for them, an instrument, a hammer. Their "knowing" is *creating*, their creating is a legislation, their will to truth is – *will to power*.[232]

Throughout history, the task of these genuine philosophers was always to be "the bad conscience of their time." Their enemy was the ideal of their time. "By applying the knife vivisectionally to the chest of the very *virtues of their time*, they betrayed what was their own secret: to know of a *new* greatness of man, of a new untrodden way to his enhancement [*Vergrösserung*]."[233] In our time, the genuine philosopher, like Nietzsche, is the bad conscience of the age of equality.

> Today, conversely, when only the herd animal receives and dispenses honors in Europe, when "equality of rights" could all too easily be changed into equality in violating rights – I mean, into a common war on all that is rare, strange, privileged, the higher man, the higher soul, the higher duty, the higher responsibility, and the abundance of creative power and masterfulness – today the concept of greatness entails

being noble, wanting to be by oneself, being able to be different, standing alone and having to live independently. And the philosopher will betray something of his own ideal when he posits: "He shall be greatest who can be loneliest, the most concealed, the most deviant, the human being beyond good and evil, the master of his virtues, he that is overrich in will. Precisely this shall be called *greatness:* being capable of being as manifold as whole, as ample as full." And to ask it once more: today – is greatness *possible?*[234]

As the bad conscience of our time, Nietzsche demonstrated his own greatness by applying his knife (i.e., the revaluation of all values) vivisectionally to the chest of the virtues (i.e., slave values) of the age of equality and in the process revealed a new concept of human greatness (i.e., a new nobility) and a new untrodden way to human enhancement (i.e., the higher breeding of humanity). This project of human enhancement also has a religious aspect that Nietzsche expressed in his concept of Dionysus.

---

[1] *Beyond Good and Evil* is subtitled *Prelude to a Philosophy of the Future.* It was a prelude because Nietzsche planned to publish the philosophy of the future in a four-volume *magnum opus* with the title of *The Will to Power: Attempt at a Revaluation of All Values.* Young, *Nietzsche*, 407. See n. 30 on p. 37 and cited text on p. 34 above.

[2] "All credibility, all good conscience, all evidence of truth come only from the senses." BGE, §134.

[3] Nietzsche abandoned metaphysical idealism before or during the writing of his fourth *Untimely Meditation.* Young, *Nietzsche*, 221.

[4] HA I, §9.

[5] Z I, Prologue, §3.

[6] TI III, §2.

[7] EH, Preface, §2.

[8] TI IV. The longest error was the invention of a "real world." Ibid.

[9] Lampert, *Nietzsche's Teaching*, 21.

[10] Z I, Prologue, §3.

[11] Z I, Prologue, §6.

[12] Z I, On the Despisers of the Body.

[13] Z III, The Convalescent, §2.

[14] A, §43. "So far as the promotion of knowledge is concerned, mankind's most useful achievement is perhaps the abandonment of its belief in an immortal soul." D, §501.

[15] A, §43. "That, as an 'immortal soul,' everybody is equal to everybody else, that in the totality of beings the 'salvation' of *every* single one is permitted to claim to be of everlasting moment, that little bigots and three-quarters madmen are permitted to imagine that for their sakes the laws of nature are continually being *broken* – such a raising of every sort of egoism to infinity, to *impudence*, cannot be branded with sufficient contempt." Ibid.

[16] Z I, On the Afterworldly.

[17] HA I, §5.

[18] EH-GM.

[19] GM III, §21.

[20] TI IX, §47.

[21] See chap. 2, sect. B, subsect. 1, above.

[22] GS, §108.

[23] GS, §109. "Naturalize" is used here in the sense of naturalism, the opposite of supernaturalism.

[24] BGE, §230.

[25] Lampert, *Nietzsche's Teaching*, 178. "We speak of nature and forget to include ourselves: we ourselves are nature, *quand même* ["nonetheless"]." HA II2, §327.

[26] EH II, §10.

[27] EH IV, §8.

[28] EH III, §5.

[29] TI III, §6. Nietzsche always used the French word for decadence, but some translators replace Nietzsche's French with the English word.

[30] BGE, §259. The will to power "means 'will for power': a will to power is a will such that the thing willed is power." Rüdiger Bittner, introduction to Friedrich Nietzsche, *Writings from the Late Notebooks*, ed. Rüdiger Bittner and trans. Kate Sturge (Cambridge: Cambridge University Press, 2003), xviii. In other words, the will to power is the will to more power. Young, *Nietzsche*, 538.

[31] Z II, On Self-Overcoming.

[32] GM II, §12.

[33] BGE, §186.

[34] BGE, §36.

[35] BGE, §13.

[36] GS, §349.

[37] TI IX, §14.

[38] Z II, On Self-Overcoming.

[39] GS, §13.

[40] BGE, §259.

[41] Ibid.

[42] GM II, §18.

[43] BGE, §9.

[44] Laurence Lampert, *Nietzsche's Task: An Interpretation of "Beyond Good and Evil"* (New Haven: Yale University Press, 2001), 36.

[45] A, §6.

[46] TI IX, §37.

[47] GM III, §25. Nietzsche characterized modern democracy "as the *decaying form* of the state." TI IX, §39. "Democracy has always been the declining form of the power to organize." Ibid. "Modern democracy is the historical form of the *decay of the state.*" HA I, §472. Liberal institutions "undermine the will to power, they are the leveling of mountain and valley exalted to a moral principle, they make small, cowardly and smug – it is the herd animal which triumphs with them every time. Liberalism: in plain words, *reduction to the herd animal.*" TI IX, §38. The modern concept of equality "belongs essentially to decline." TI IX, §37. The "religion of pity" is, of course, Christianity. A, §7. Pity "is considered a virtue only among decadents." EH I, §4. The will to power is "*lacking* in all the supreme values of mankind" (i.e., Christian morality), which are "values of decline, *nihilistic* values." A, §6. Christianity is a "nihilistic" and a "*décadence*" religion. A, §20. Nietzsche took the Christian "overestimation of goodness and benevolence on a large scale for a consequence of decadence, for a symptom of weakness, irreconcilable with an ascending, Yes-saying life." EH IV, §4.

[48] A, §17.

[49] See, for example, TI IX, §35; A, §11; A, §15; EH-D, §2.

[50] TI II, §11.

[51] TI IX, §33. "At the risk of displeasing innocent ears I propose: egoism belongs to the nature of a noble soul – I mean that unshakable faith that to a being such as 'we are' other beings must be subordinate by nature and have to sacrifice themselves." BGE, §265.

[52] CW, Epilogue.

[53] Ibid.

[54] Ibid.

[55] Ibid.

[56] Ibid.

[57] A, §55.

[58] A, §17.

[59] A, §24.

[60] GM III, §18.

[61] A, §2.

[62] A, §57.

[63] GM I, Note. Nietzsche always favored the strong over the weak because strength (both physical and spiritual) is a sign of power.

[64] EH IV, §3.

[65] EH IV, §2. "It goes without saying that I do not deny – unless I am a fool – that many actions called immoral ought to be avoided and resisted, or that many called moral ought to be done and encouraged – but I think the one should be encouraged and the other avoided *for other reasons than hitherto.* We have to *learn to think differently* – in order at last, perhaps very late on, to attain even more: *to feel differently.*" D, §103.

[66] EH IV, §4.

[67] EH IV, §6.

[68] GS, §107.

[69] TI VII, §1.

[70] BGE, §108.

[71] BT, Attempt at a Self-Criticism, §5.

[72] BGE, §56. "When man no longer regards himself as evil he ceases to be so!" D, §148.

[73] EH IV, §4.

[74] GM, Preface, §6.

[75] Ibid.

[76] GS, §1.

[77] GS, §4. "To be evil is 'not to act in accordance with custom,' to practice things not sanctioned by custom, to resist tradition, however rational or stupid that tradition may be." HA I, §96.

[78] GS, §4. "The frightful energies – those which are called evil – are the cyclopean architects and road-makers of humanity." HA I, §246.

[79] Z I, Prologue, §9.

[80] GS, §4.

[81] EH IV, §4.

[82] Ibid. (quoting Z III, On Old and New Tablets, §26).

[83] Z I, Prologue, §9.

[84] EH IV, §5.

[85] Ibid. Here Nietzsche paraphrases Zarathustra: "You highest men [i.e., the good and just] whom my eyes have seen, this is my doubt concerning you and my secret laughter: I guess that you would call my overman – devil." Z II, On Human Prudence.

[86] Z III, On Old and New Tablets, §2.

[87] Z I, On the Thousand and One Goals.

[88] Z II, On Self-Overcoming. Change is "the very essence of immorality." GM III, §9.

[89] Z III, The Convalescent, §2.

[90] Z IV, On the Higher Man, §5. "Perhaps some future survey of the requirements of mankind will show that it is absolutely not desirable that all men should act in the same way, but rather that in the interest of ecumenical goals whole tracts of mankind ought to have special, perhaps under certain circumstances even evil tasks imposed upon them." HA I, §25.

[91] Z III, On Old and New Tablets, §29. Except for minor variations, this section is repeated at the end of *Twilight of the Idols* where it is called "The Hammer Speaks." TI XI.

[92] EH-Z, §8.

[93] Z III, On Old and New Tablets, §12.

[94] EH-BT, §4. Kaufmann's translation has been modified. See n. 39 on p. 37 above.

[95] BGE, §257.

[96] Z III, On Old and New Tablets, §11.

[97] Z III, On Old and New Tablets, §12.

[98] Ibid.

[99] EH-BGE, §2. Elsewhere in *Ecce Homo*, Nietzsche described a test for nobility.

"The first point on which I 'try the reins' is to see whether a man has a feeling for distance in his system, whether he sees rank, degree, order between man and man everywhere, whether he makes *distinctions*: with that one is a *gentilhomme* ["nobleman"]; otherwise one belongs hopelessly in the broad-minded – ah, so good-natured – concept of canaille." EH-CW, §4.

[100] Lampert, *Nietzsche's Task*, 262.

[101] Z III, On Old and New Tablets, §11.

[102] GS, §377. Slavery is also "a condition of every higher culture, every enhancement of culture." BGE, §239. In Nietzsche's view, there are very few non-slaves. "As at all times, so now too, men are divided into the slaves and the free; for he who does not have two-thirds of his day to himself is a slave, let him be what he may otherwise: statesman, businessman, official, scholar." HA I, §283.

[103] BGE, §257.

[104] Ibid.

[105] Ibid. "I employed the word 'state': it is obvious what is meant – some pack of blond beasts of prey, a conqueror and master race which, organized for war and with the ability to organize, unhesitatingly lays its terrible claws upon a populace perhaps tremendously superior in numbers but still formless and nomad. That is after all how the 'state' began on earth: I think that sentimentalism which would have it begin with a 'contract' has been disposed of. He who can command, he who is by nature 'master,' he who is violent in act and bearing – what has he to do with contracts!" GM II, §17.

[106] A, §57. In this section, Nietzsche used the Law of Manu as an example of a "good law-book" that "summarizes the experience, policy and experimental morality of long centuries." Ibid.

[107] Ibid.

[108] Z III, On Old and New Tablets, §21.

[109] A, §57.

[110] GS, §358.

[111] A, §57. "To be a public utility, a cog, a function, is a natural vocation [. . .] For the mediocre it is happiness to be mediocre." Ibid.

[112] Ibid. "Injustice never lies in unequal rights, it lies in the claim to '*equal*' rights." Ibid. "'Equality for equals, inequality for unequals' – *that* would be the true voice of justice: and, what follows from it, 'Never make equal what is unequal.'" TI IX, §48. Or, as Zarathustra says, "For, to *me* justice speaks thus: 'Men are not equal.' Nor shall they become equal!" Z II, On the Tarantulas.

[113] BGE, §258.

[114] BGE, §257.

[115] EH-BT, §4. Kaufmann's translation has been modified. See n. 39 on p. 37 above.

[116] UM II, §9. Instead of *Züchtung*, Nietzsche used in his *Untimely Meditations* the words "*Erzeugung*" and "*Entstehung*," which were translated by Hollingdale as "production" or "procreation."

[117] Ibid.

[118] UM III, §5.

[119] UM III, §3.

[120] UM III, §6.

[121] GM III, §14. See passage quoted at n. 144 on p. 81 below.

[122] UM III, §6.

[123] A, §3. See passage quoted at n. 142 on p. 81 below.

[124] UM III, §6.

[125] HA I, §24.

[126] D, §108. Nietzsche continued, "But up to now the moral law has been supposed to stand *above* our own likes and dislikes: one did not want actually to *impose* this law upon oneself, one wanted to *take* it from somewhere or *discover* it somewhere or *have it commanded to one* from somewhere." Ibid.

[127] WLN, 9[153]. Nietzsche explained, "The progressive diminishment of man is what drives one to think about the breeding of a *stronger race*, a race whose surplus would lie precisely in those areas where the diminished species was becoming weak and weaker (will, responsibility, self-assurance, the capacity to set itself goals)." Ibid.

[128] BGE, §225.

[129] See n. 39 on p. 37 above for the meaning of the noun *Züchtung*. The verb *züchten* means "to breed" animals or people, "to keep" bees, "to grow" or "to cultivate" plants, or "to cultivate" pearls or bacteria. *Langenscheidt*, s.v. "züchten."

[130] Richardson, *Nietzsche's New Darwinism*, 192-93.

[131] BGE, §262. Depending upon the context, Kaufmann translated *Züchtung* as either "breeding" or "cultivation" and *züchten* as either "to breed" or "to cultivate."

[132] Ibid.

[133] Richardson, *Nietzsche's New Darwinism*, 84. See, for example, BGE, §213, and BGE, §264.

[134] Richardson, *Nietzsche's New Darwinism*, 18. "Education is a continuation of procreation, and often a kind of supplementary beautification of it." D, §397.

[135] Richardson, *Nietzsche's New Darwinism*, 192-93.

[136] Ibid., 193.

[137] Ibid.

[138] BGE, §61. Kaufmann's translation of *Züchtung* has been changed from "cultivation" to "breeding."

[139] BGE, §62. Kaufmann's translation of *Züchtung* has been changed from "cultivation" to "breeding."

[140] BGE, §188; BGE, §203. Kaufmann's translation of *Züchtung* has been changed from "cultivation" to "breeding." "*Zucht und Züchtung*" is also the title of Book Four of *The Will to Power* but translated there by Kaufmann as "Discipline and Breeding" instead of "discipline and cultivation" as he did in *Beyond Good and Evil*.

[141] TI IX, §51.

[142] A, §3.

[143] Instead of "overman" like Kaufmann, Hollingdale translated *Übermensch* as "superman."

[144] A, §4. The use of Overman in this context can be explained by Nietzsche's formula for greatness in a human being and this formula's relationship with the

idea of the eternal recurrence. See chap. 7 below.

145 A, §3.

146 A, §5.

147 A, §4. See also WP, §684.

148 A, §14. "Formerly one sought the feeling of the grandeur of man by pointing to his divine *origin*: this has now become a forbidden way, for at its portal stands the ape, together with other gruesome beasts, grinning knowingly as if to say: no further in this direction!" D, §49.

149 A, §14.

150 GM II, §16.

151 BGE, §62.

152 TI IX, §14.

153 WLN, 14[123].

154 "The goal of Nietzsche's politics is the enhancement or heightening (*Erhöhung*) of the type human, an enhancement achieved by individual souls. Aristocratic society and the slavery it presupposes are instrumental necessities, preconditions of the true aim, the aristocratic individual." Lampert, *Nietzsche's Task*, 264.

155 "Nietzsche's redesign of society establishes a functional relation among these three groups: the herd is mainly designed for the sake of the elite, who are mainly designed for the sake of the exceptions." Richardson, *Nietzsche's New Darwinism*, 206.

156 BGE, §258.

157 See chap. 5, sect. D, above.

158 D, §272.

159 There is evidence that Nietzsche had read Francis Galton's *Inquiries into Human Faculty and Its Development* (1883) in which Galton invented the term eugenics. Curtis Cate, *Friedrich Nietzsche* (Woodstock, N.Y.: Overlook Press, 2002), 448; *Conversations with Nietzsche*, 152-53. According to one acquaintance, Nietzsche "admired" Galton "so very much." Ibid., 153.

160 Richardson, *Nietzsche's New Darwinism*, 146.

161 "Marriage in the aristocratic sense, the old nobility's sense of the word, is about *breeding* a race (is there still a nobility today? Quaeritur ["one asks"]), in other words about maintaining a fixed, particular type of ruling men: man and woman were sacrificed to this viewpoint. [. . .] this noble concept of marriage [. . .] has ruled in every healthy aristocracy, in ancient Athens as in eighteenth-century Europe." WLN, 4[6].

162 HA I, §243.

163 HA II1, §278.

164 D, §150. For specific recommendations of eugenic methods, see WP, §733.

165 Z I, On Child and Marriage. "For the individual, the 'single man,' as people and philosophers have hitherto understood him, is an error: he does not constitute a separate entity, an atom, a 'link in the chain,' something merely inherited from the past – he constitutes the entire *single* line 'man' up to and including himself." TI IX, §33. The idea expressed here that an individual is the sum of the genes inherited from both parents, which they have inherited from their parents, and so on,

explains Nietzsche's belief in the importance of eugenics. Young, *Nietzsche*, 499.

[166] Z III, On Old and New Tablets, §24.

[167] See chap. 4, sect. E, above.

[168] TI VII, §§1-5.

[169] TI VII, §2.

[170] WP, §398. Reflecting Nietzsche's standard of value, the strong man (both physically and spiritually) is more valuable than the weak man because the former has more power than the latter.

[171] TI VII, §2. See chap. 2, sect. A, subsect. 2, above.

[172] TI VII, §3.

[173] Ibid.

[174] Ibid.

[175] "Perhaps there is nothing which outrages our feelings more than *these* protective measures of Indian morality." Ibid. "These regulations are instructive enough: in them we find for once *Aryan* humanity, quite pure, quite primordial – we learn that the concept 'pure blood' is the opposite of a harmless concept." TI VII, §4.

[176] A, §56.

[177] See n. 106 on p. 101 and cited text on p. 75 above.

[178] This identification of the European problem helps to explain Nietzsche's critical comments about German nationalism. These comments increased after June 1888 when the more liberal and humane Kaiser Friedrich III died of cancer after a reign of only 99 days and was succeeded by the more nationalistic and bellicose Kaiser Wilhelm II. On 20 June 1888, Nietzsche wrote a friend, "The death of Kaiser Friedrich has moved me: in the end he was a small glimmering light of *free* thought, the last hope for Germany. Now the rule of *Stöcker* [the leading German Christian anti-Semite of the time] begins." Quoted in Friedrich Nietzsche, *On the Genealogy of Morals* and *Ecce Homo,* trans. Walter Kaufmann and R. J. Hollingdale (New York: Vintage Books, 1967), 297, n. 6. For an explanation of Nietzsche's negative opinion of Christian anti-Semitism, see n. 89 on p. 29 above.

[179] EH-CW, §2. At the end of this section, Nietzsche asked, "Does anyone besides me know the way out of this dead-end street? – A task that is great enough to *unite* nations again?" Ibid.

[180] HA II2, §87. Nietzsche used the phrase "good Europeans" to describe himself and others whose perspective and interests transcended the national to encompass the European. HA I, §475; GS, §377. His idea of what encompassed European culture and society included the European overseas settlements. HA II2, §215.

[181] BGE, §251. The complete sentence reads: "But here it is proper to break off my cheerful Germanomania and holiday oratory; for I am beginning to touch on what is *serious* for me, the 'European problem' as I understand it, the cultivation of a new caste that will rule Europe." Ibid.

[182] Ibid.

[183] BGE, §256. Part of Nietzsche's admiration for Napoleon stemmed from his belief that Napoleon "brought back again a whole slab of antiquity" that might "finally become master again over the national movement" and "become the heir and continuator of Napoleon in an *affirmative* sense; for what he wanted was one

unified Europe, as is known – as *mistress of the earth.*" GS, §362. The "miracle of meaning in the existence of Napoleon" was that he was "a *force majeure* ["superior force"] of genius and will [who] became visible, strong enough to create a unity of Europe, a political and *economic* unity for the sake of a world government." EH-CW, §2. In a letter to a friend in October 1888, Nietzsche wrote that Napoleon was "the only man hitherto strong enough to make Europe into a political and *economic unity.*" Nietzsche, *Selected Letters*, 315.

184 BGE, §208.

185 Ibid.

186 D, §272.

187 BGE, §200.

188 HA I, §475.

189 BGE, §242.

190 HA I, §475.

191 BGE, §251.

192 Ibid.

193 D, §272.

194 GM I, §5.

195 Ibid. Nietzsche thought that the Germans were "a people of the most monstrous mixture and medley of races, perhaps even with a preponderance of the pre-Aryan element." BGE, §244.

196 EH-BT, §4.

197 "The dangerous anti-natural character of Christianity [. . .] thwarts *natural selection.*" WLN, 14[5].

198 GM II, §12.

199 WP, §679. "A people is a detour of nature to get to six or seven great men. – Yes, and then to get around them." BGE, §126.

200 WP, §681. "*Basic error*: to place the goal in the herd and not in single individuals! The herd is a means, no more!" WP, §766.

201 WP, §760. "The well-being of the majority and the well-being of the few are opposite viewpoints of value: to consider the former *a priori* of higher value may be left to the naïveté of English biologists." GM I, Note.

202 TI IX, §36. "The invalid is a parasite on society. In a certain state it is indecent to go on living. To vegetate on in cowardly dependence on physicians and medicaments after the meaning of life, the *right* to life, has been lost ought to entail the profound contempt of society." Ibid.

203 HA I, §30.

204 WP, §734. See also GS, §73, entitled "Holy cruelty."

205 A, §2.

206 A, §5.

207 Richardson, *Nietzsche's New Darwinism*, 142.

208 A, §7.

209 See chap. 2, sect. A, subsect. 1, above.

210 BGE, §62.

211 EH IV, §8. Although "the German Kaiser calls it his 'Christian duty' to liberate

the slaves in Africa," Nietzsche called it "psychological depravity." EH-CW, §3. Nietzsche took "Negroes [. . .] as representatives of prehistoric man." GM II, §7.

212 A, §43. "None of these ponderous herd animals [. . .] wants to know [. . .] that what is fair for one *cannot* by any means for that reason alone also be fair for others; that the demand of one morality for all is detrimental for the higher men; in short, that there is an order of rank between man and man, hence also between morality and morality." BGE, §228.
213 TI IX, §37.
214 A, §43.
215 Ibid.
216 WP, §464.
217 WP, §246.
218 See chap. 5, sect. D, above.
219 BGE, §42.
220 Lampert, *Nietzsche's Task*, 94.
221 BGE, §44.
222 EH-HA, §1.
223 BGE, §44. Nietzsche called himself a free, very free spirit. BGE, Preface.
224 BGE, §44.
225 Ibid.
226 BGE, §225.
227 BGE, §44.
228 BGE, §203.
229 Ibid. The democratization of Europe will lead "to the leveling and mediocritization of man – to a useful, industrious, handy, multi-purpose herd animal." BGE, §242.
230 BGE, §211.
231 BGE, §261.
232 BGE, §211.
233 BGE, §212.
234 Ibid.

Chapter 6

DIONYSUS

Nietzsche's project of human enhancement is not only a political project, it is also a religious project. Just as the idea of the eternal recurrence provides the basis of his philosophy of the future, it also provides the basis of the religion of the future. Nietzsche "baptized" this "highest of all possible faiths" with the name Dionysus.[1]

Nietzsche expressed the concept of Dionysus and the underlying idea of the eternal recurrence in various ways. As the Overman (i.e., one who overcomes humanity by willing the eternal recurrence of all things), Zarathustra embodied the concept of Dionysus. Nietzsche himself also embodied the Dionysian concept through his *amor fati* ("love of fate"), an idea that is almost identical to the idea of the eternal recurrence.

Nietzsche also expressed his embodiment of the concept of Dionysus in religious terms. He called himself an "initiate" and "disciple" of the "god" and "philosopher" Dionysus as well as identified himself with Dionysus in various ways to include using the term "Antichrist" to refer to both himself and Dionysus.

With the idea of the eternal recurrence and its expression in the concept of Dionysus, Nietzsche intended to provide if not a new religious faith to replace Christian faith, then at least a semi-religious philosophical substitute for Christianity. He wanted to provide the philosophical basis for a new religion, much like Plato had done for Christianity. He expressed this intent in the phrase "Dionysus versus the Crucified." Nietzsche called on philosophers of the future to use this new Dionysian faith in their project of human enhancement.

A. Return of Dionysus

One of Nietzsche's major themes throughout his works was the necessity for the "world-historical" event of the "return of the Greek spirit."[2] He intended to bring back the Greek spirit in his concept of Dionysus.

In *The Birth of Tragedy* (1872), Nietzsche argued that Greek tragedy was born from "the tremendous phenomenon of the Dionysian," but tragedy then died from "the Socratism of morality, the dialectics, frugality, and cheerfulness of the theoretical man."[3] At the time of writing this book, Nietzsche saw in the Wagnerian opera "the phenomenon of the reawakening of the Dionysian spirit and the rebirth of tragedy,"[4] which would inspire a new cultural renaissance.[5] Although he later broke with Wagner, the Wagnerian ideal of the redemption of European culture through the rebirth of "the Greek," aided by art and religion, remained central to Nietzsche's thinking about art, religion, and society until the end.[6]

In *Ecce Homo*, Nietzsche wrote that a "tremendous hope speaks out of" *The Birth of Tragedy*. "In the end I lack all reason to renounce the hope for a Dionysian future of music." He also revealed that everything in his essay *Richard Wagner in Bayreuth* (1876) points to "the impending return of the Greek spirit, the necessity of counter-Alexanders who will retie the Gordian knot of Greek culture."[7] He also noted that "the idea of Bayreuth" – the Wagnerian ideal – was later transformed "into something that should not puzzle those who know my *Zarathustra*: into that great noon at which the most elect consecrate themselves for the greatest of all tasks. Who could say? The vision of a feast that I shall yet live to see."[8]

With the defeat of the greatest Socratic, Plato, in *Thus Spoke Zarathustra*,[9] Dionysus, the god of tragedy, and the Greek spirit can now return.[10] Although Dionysus is not revealed by name in *Zarathustra*, Zarathustra indicates a role for the Greek god in the Great Noon by preparing for his return.[11] Zarathustra's songs in the book's climax at the end of the third part anticipate the return of Dionysus, "the god of tragedy, the earthly god of earthly life."[12] After his redemption, Zarathustra sings of "the nameless one for whom only future songs will find names"[13] and of "a golden boat [. . .] on nocturnal waters."[14] Dionysus is the "nameless one"[15] and the "golden boat" is a sign of his arrival.[16]

This role for the god of tragedy explains the title, "*Incipit tragoedia*" ("The tragedy begins"), of the last section of the first edition of *The Gay Science*,[17] which, except for a few words, is identical to the first section of "Zarathustra's Prologue," which begins Nietzsche's next book. Also, he wrote that in the period just before writing *Zarathustra* "the Yes-saying pathos *par excellence*, which I call the tragic pathos, was alive in me to the highest degree."[18] *Zarathustra* is his tragedy in which he prepared for the return of Dionysus. Because tragedy is "the highest art in saying Yes to life,"[19] Dionysus, as the god of tragedy, later becomes Nietzsche's symbol for the idea of the eternal recurrence, as we shall see in the next section.[20]

After Nietzsche prepared for the literary return of Dionysus in the tragedy called *Zarathustra*, Dionysus, along with his consort Ariadne, did return in the penultimate section of Nietzsche's next book, *Beyond Good and Evil*. Through the mouth of Dionysus, Nietzsche asserted that humanity must become "stronger, more evil, and more profound."

> "Under certain circumstances I love what is human" – and with this he alluded to Ariadne who was present – "man is to my mind an agreeable, courageous, inventive animal that has no equal on earth; it finds its way in any labyrinth. I am well disposed towards him: I often reflect how I might yet advance [*vorwärts bringen*] him and make him stronger, more evil, and more profound than he is."
>
> "Stronger, more evil, and more profound?" I asked startled. "Yes," he said once more; "stronger, more evil, and more profound; also more beautiful" – and at that the tempter god [*Versucher-Gott*] smiled with his halcyon smile as though he had just paid an enchanting compliment. Here we also see: what this divinity lacks is not only a sense of shame – and there are also other good reasons for conjecturing that in several respects all of the gods could learn from us humans. We humans are – more humane. –[21]

Although Dionysus first appears by name in *Beyond Good and Evil*, the concept of Dionysus was already present in *Zarathustra* because Zarathustra, as the Overman, embodies the concept of the Dionysian.

B. Zarathustra as Dionysian Overman

In an illuminating section in *Ecce Homo*, Nietzsche described the concepts of the Overman and the Dionysian as virtually identical and described both concepts as being embodied by Zarathustra. Not only did Nietzsche's concept of the Overman become, as noted earlier,[22] "the greatest reality" in Zarathustra, but his concept of the Dionysian had also become "a *supreme deed*"[23] in Zarathustra. Although redundant, Zarathustra can, therefore, be called a Dionysian Overman.[24]

Nietzsche declared that his "concept of the 'Dionysian' here [in *Zarathustra*] became a *supreme deed*." It became a supreme deed when Zarathustra overcame humanity by willing the eternal recurrence of all things to become the Overman. The concept of the Overman, therefore, includes the concept of the Dionysian. As the "most Yes-saying of all spirits,"[25] Zarathustra, the Dionysian Overman, wills the eternal recurrence of all things and thus effectuates the "highest formula of affirmation that is at all attainable."[26]

As the Overman, "Zarathustra experiences himself as the *supreme type of all beings*"[27] that he defines as "the highest species of all being"[28] in the decisive chapter "On Old and New Tablets," which Nietzsche quoted in *Ecce Homo*.

"The soul that has the longest ladder and reaches down deepest – the most comprehensive soul, which can run and stray and roam farthest within itself; the most necessary soul that plunges joyously into chance; the soul that, having being, dives into becoming; the soul that *has*, but *wants* to want and will; the soul that flees itself and catches up with itself in the widest circles; the wisest soul that folly exhorts most sweetly; the soul that loves itself most, in which all things have their sweep and countersweep and ebb and flood – "[29]

"But," Nietzsche immediately declared, *"that is the concept of Dionysus him-self."*[30] Just like the Overman, Dionysus is the supreme type of all be-ings with "the most comprehensive soul."

Furthermore, the apparent contradiction of saying and doing No while being a Yes-saying spirit is characteristic of Zarathustra as well as of Dionysus. In Zarathustra, "all opposites are blended into a new unity."[31]

> The psychological problem in the type of Zarathustra is how he that says No and *does* No to an unheard-of degree, to everything to which one has so far said Yes, can nevertheless be the opposite of a No-saying spirit; how the spirit who bears the heaviest fate, a fatality of a task, can nevertheless be the lightest and most trans-cendent – Zarathustra is a dancer – how he that has the hardest, most terrible insight into reality, that has thought the "most abysmal idea," nevertheless does not consider it an objection to existence, not even to its eternal recurrence – but rather one reason more for being himself the eternal Yes to all things, "the tremen-dous, unbounded saying Yes and Amen." – "Into all abysses I still carry the blessings of my saying Yes." – *But this is the concept of Dionysus once again.*[32]

The "most abysmal idea" is, of course, the idea of the eternal re-currence. As this is *"the concept of Dionysus once again,"* the idea of the eternal recurrence is not only the "doctrine of Zarathustra,"[33] it is also the concept of Dionysus.[34]

Nietzsche equated the type of Zarathustra with not only the Over-man but also with Dionysus. The concept of the Overman had become the greatest reality in Zarathustra at the same time that the concept of Dionysus had become a supreme deed in Zarathustra. Both events oc-curred when Zarathustra overcame humanity by willing the eternal re-currence of all things. In overcoming humanity, Zarathustra attains re-demption. Instead of using the term redemption, Nietzsche expressed his own redemption with the phrase *amor fati.*

C. *Amor Fati*

To Nietzsche, the Dionysian idea of the eternal recurrence was more than just an important philosophical idea. It was personal. It was expressed in his "inmost nature" as *amor fati* ("love of fate").[35] Through *amor fati*, Nietzsche overcame his own nausea over humanity, thereby attaining redemption and becoming the Overman himself, although he never admitted so by using that term.[36] Presumably including himself as one of the great, he also used *amor fati* as his formula for greatness in a human being.[37]

Nietzsche claimed that he "became the first to comprehend the wonderful phenomenon of the Dionysian" because it was "the only parable and parallel in history" for his "own inmost experience."[38] He expressed this "inmost experience" with the words "*amor fati*." He revealed the link between the concept of Dionysus and *amor fati* in his notes of 1888 when he wrote that his "formula" for standing "in a Dionysian relationship to existence" is *amor fati*, which is the "highest state a philosopher can attain."[39]

Nietzsche first used the expression *amor fati* in the first section of the fourth book of *The Gay Science* (written in January 1882), only a few months after the idea of the eternal recurrence came to him.

> *For the new year.* – I still live, I still think: I still have to live, for I still have to think. *Sum, ergo cogito: cogito, ergo sum* ["I am, therefore I think: I think, therefore I am"]. Today everybody permits himself the expression of his wish and his dearest thought; hence I, too, shall say what it is that I wish from myself today, and what was the first thought to run across my heart this year – what thought shall be for me the reason, warranty, and sweetness of my life henceforth. I want to learn more and more to see as beautiful what is necessary in things; then I shall be one of those who make things beautiful. *Amor fati*: let that be my love henceforth! I do not want to wage war against what is ugly. I do not want to accuse; I do not even want to accuse those who accuse. *Looking away* shall be my only negation. And all in all and on the whole: some day I wish to be only a Yes-sayer.[40]

As Nietzsche described *amor fati* here and in his later books, the concept is almost identical to the idea of the eternal recurrence. The difference is in scope. While the idea of the eternal recurrence requires the willing of the eternal recurrence of all things, *amor fati* requires the willing of the eternal recurrence of only one's own life, that is, saying Yes to everything that has contributed to one's life up to the present moment. It is a matter of "accepting oneself as if fated, not wishing oneself 'different.'"[41] Nonetheless, willing the eternal recurrence of one's own life necessarily means that one also wills the eternal recurrence of all things. One's own life cannot eternally recur if all things do not also eternally recur. Nietzsche expressed this idea in his notes.

> If we say Yes to a single moment, this means we have said Yes not only to ourselves, but to all existence. For nothing stands alone, either in us ourselves or in things: and if just once our soul has quivered and resounded with happiness like a harpstring, then all eternity was needed to condition that one event – and in that one moment of our saying Yes, all eternity was welcomed, redeemed, justified and affirmed.[42]

As already discussed,[43] this kind of willing redeems one from nausea over humanity. Like Zarathustra, Nietzsche suffered from nausea over humanity and pity for humanity. He called "the *great nausea at man!*" and the "*great pity for man!*" the "two worst contagions" reserved just for him and his "friends."[44] In *Ecce Homo*, Nietzsche wrote, "*Nausea* over man, over the 'rabble,' was always my greatest danger,"[45] and "*Nausea* at man is my danger."[46] By 1888, he had overcome his nausea over humanity.

Between 1882 and 1888, Nietzsche progressed from wishing to be "only a Yes-sayer" to actually being a Yes-sayer and one who loves his own fate. On his forty-fourth birthday – "this perfect day,"[47] Nietzsche expressed his *amor fati* and celebrated his Dionysian affirmation of life by commencing work on *Ecce Homo*.

> I looked back, I looked forward, and never saw so many and such good things at once. It was not for nothing that I buried my forty-fourth year today; I had the *right* to bury it; whatever

113

was life in it has been saved, is immortal. The first book of the *Revaluation of All Values* [*The Anti-Christ*], the *Songs of Zar-athustra* [*Dithyrambs of Dionysus*], the *Twilight of the Idols*, my attempt to philosophize with a hammer – all presents of this year, indeed of its last quarter! *How could I fail to be grateful to my whole life?* – and so I tell my life to myself.[48]

The whole of *Ecce Homo* expresses Nietzsche's *amor fati*. He triumphed over *ressentiment* by relating the story of his life and work in a spirit of gratitude instead of bearing a grudge toward the world that had ignored him up to this point. He made no excuses and did not complain about his illness, which kept him in constant physical pain for much of his adult life, but rather expressed thankfulness and explained how it made his life better.[49] He claimed that he was "ultimately indebted" to his "protracted sickness" for his "freedom from *ressentiment*, enlightenment about *ressentiment*."[50]

Recalling in *Ecce Homo* how he became what he was without "willing" or "striving," Nietzsche wrote, "At this very moment I still look upon my future – an *ample* future! – as upon calm seas: there is no ripple of desire. I do not want in the least that anything should become different than it is; I myself do not want to become different."[51]

At the end of the same chapter, Nietzsche expanded upon this expression of *amor fati* and connected it with the key to human greatness in general and by implication with his own greatness in particular.

> My formula for greatness in a human being is *amor fati*: that one wants nothing to be different, not forward, not backward, not in all eternity. Not merely bear what is necessary, still less conceal it – all idealism is mendaciousness in the face of what is necessary – but *love* it.[52]

Reflecting his own greatness, Nietzsche affirmed that "what is *necessary* does not hurt me; *amor fati* is my inmost nature."[53] In the epilogue of his last book, *Nietzsche contra Wagner* (written in December 1888), Nietzsche again affirmed that *amor fati* is his inmost nature.

I have often asked myself whether I am not more heavily obligated to the hardest years of my life than to any others. As my inmost nature teaches me, whatever is necessary – as seen from the heights and in the sense of a *great* economy – is also the useful par excellence: one should not only bear it, one should *love* it. *Amor fati*: that is my inmost nature. And as for my long sickness, do I not owe it indescribably more than I owe to my health? I owe it a *higher* health – one which is made stronger by whatever does not kill it. *I also owe my philosophy to it.*[54]

Amor fati was Nietzsche's expression for his own Dionysian affirmation of life in which he willed the eternal recurrence of his own life and said Yes to everything that had contributed to his life up to the present moment. By willing the eternal recurrence of his own life, he also willed the eternal recurrence of all things. By doing so, Nietzsche overcame his nausea over humanity and thus attained redemption. Like Zarathustra, Nietzsche embodied the concept of Dionysus as the Overman.

D. Nietzsche as Disciple of Dionysus

In addition to *amor fati*, Nietzsche expressed his embodiment of the concept of Dionysus in religious terms. As already mentioned,[55] he used the term "redemption" (*die Erlösung*) to refer to Zarathustra's task as well as his own task.[56] Also, he not only called himself an "initiate" and "disciple" of the "god" and "philosopher" Dionysus, but the ambiguities in some of his last writings indicate that Nietzsche eventually identified himself *as* Dionysus.

In his first book after *Zarathustra*, *Beyond Good and Evil* (1886), Nietzsche called himself "the last disciple and initiate of the god Dionysus."[57] Writing in 1886, he again called himself "the initiate and disciple of his god"[58] in his new introduction to *The Birth of Tragedy* entitled "Attempt at a Self-Criticism." At the end of *Twilight of the Idols* (written in 1888), he called himself not only "the teacher of the eternal recurrence," but also, in the same sentence, "the last disciple of the philosopher Dionysus."[59] Finally, in the preface to *Ecce Homo* (written in

1888), Nietzsche declared, "I am a disciple of the philosopher Diony-sus; I should prefer to be even a satyr to being a saint."[60]

In *Ecce Homo*, Nietzsche quoted the section of *Beyond Good and Evil* where he called himself "the last disciple and initiate of the god Dio-nysus" as a "curious bit of psychology" to give an idea of himself as a "psychologist." Forbidding the reader to surmise about whom he is describing in the passage, Nietzsche only quoted the beginning of the section, where Dionysus is called the "genius of the heart" and "the tempter god [*Versucher-Gott*] and born pied piper of consciences" with-out being identified by name.[61] The reader is left to guess whether Nie-tzsche intended to describe himself or the unnamed Dionysus or both.

Nietzsche also identified himself with Dionysus through his po-etry. In one of his lesser known books, *Dithyrambs of Dionysus*, he pub-lished nine poems, three of which had already appeared in *Zarathustra*. The poems were composed from 1883 to 1888 and then collected to-gether for publication by Nietzsche in the summer of 1888.[62] In its primary meaning, a dithyramb is "a Greek choric hymn to Dionysus."[63] The title of this book means that Nietzsche had assumed the role of the poet of Dionysus. This meaning is confirmed in the section in *Ecce Homo* immediately after the section discussed in chapter 6, section B, above,[64] entitled "Zarathustra as Dionysian Overman."

> What language will such a spirit speak when he speaks to himself? The language of the *dithyramb*. I am the inventor of the dithyramb. Listen to how Zarathustra speaks to himself before sunrise: such emerald happiness, such divine tender-ness did not have a tongue before me. Even the deepest mel-ancholy of such a Dionysus still turns into a dithyramb. To give some indication of this, I choose the "Night Song," the immortal lament at being condemned by the over-abundance of light and power, by his sun-nature, not to love.[65]

Nietzsche then quoted the "Night Song" in full from *Zarathustra* and followed it in the next section with: "Nothing like this has ever been written, felt, or *suffered*: thus suffers a god, a Dionysus."[66] In this case, the reader is left to guess whether Nietzsche intended to refer to him-self or to Zarathustra or to both as Dionysus.

Shortly after writing *Ecce Homo*, Nietzsche did indeed become Dionysus in his own mind.[67] After his mental collapse on 3 January 1889, he wrote five letters to friends in which he signed with only the name "Dionysus."[68] In another letter to Cosima Wagner, the famous composer's widow, he wrote, "Ariadne, I love you. Dionysus."[69]

Along with describing himself as an initiate and disciple of Dionysus and possibly as Dionysus himself, Nietzsche also identified himself with Dionysus by referring to both himself and Dionysus as the Antichrist.

E. The Antichrist

As we shall see more fully in the next section, Nietzsche's concept of Dionysus was the direct opposite of that of Christianity. For that reason, he identified his concept of Dionysus with the Antichrist. He also associated the Antichrist with himself and his philosophy.

As a "philologist and man of words," Nietzsche claimed to have taken "some liberty" when naming the anti-Christian valuation of life that he expressed in *The Birth of Tragedy* – "for who could claim to know the rightful name of the Antichrist?" He called it Dionysian.[70] With this rhetorical question and the use of the phrase *"Dionysus versus the Crucified"*[71] at the end of *Ecce Homo*, Nietzsche intended his concept of Dionysus to represent the Antichrist. After all, "Dionysus is, as is known, also the god of darkness."[72]

Nietzsche also referred to himself as the Antichrist. As the author who condemned Christianity[73] in *The Anti-Christ*, who else could the title refer to but to Nietzsche himself? Also, the seven clauses of the "Law against Christianity" that conclude *The Anti-Christ* is signed "The Anti-Christ."[74] And probably in reference to the ass festival in *Zarathustra* (an ass was worshipped in the fourth part as if it was a god),[75] Nietzsche wrote in *Ecce Homo*, "All of us know, some even know from experience, which animal has long ears. Well then, I dare assert that I have the smallest ears. [. . .] I am the *anti-ass par excellence* and thus a world-historical monster – I am, in Greek, and not only in Greek, the *Antichrist*."[76]

Describing either himself or his philosophy, Nietzsche also made reference to the Antichrist in his private letters. After completing the first part of *Zarathustra*, he wrote in a letter to a friend, dated March

117

1883, "Do you want to know a new name for me? The language of the church *has* one – I am . . . the *Antichrist*."[77] In August of the same year, he wrote to another friend.

> I enclose the letter, also the first public statement on *Zara-thustra I*; strange to relate, the letter was written in a prison. What pleases me is to see that this first reader has at once felt what it is all about: the long-promised Antichrist. There has not been since Voltaire such an outrageous attack on Christianity – and, to tell the truth, even Voltaire had no idea that one could attack it in *this* way.[78]

In *Beyond Good and Evil*, Nietzsche described his philosophy as belonging to the Antichrist but more obliquely. In discussing "all the more profound and comprehensive men of this century," who he thought were unconsciously working toward a new unified Europe, Nietzsche concluded that unfortunately "all of them broke and collapsed in the end before the Christian cross (with right and reason: for who among them would have been profound and original enough for a philosophy of the *Antichrist*)."[79] The implication here, of course, is that Nietzsche was the only one "profound and original enough" for such a philosophy – one that could replace Christianity.

F. Dionysus Versus the Crucified

Although he did not regard himself as a "founder of a religion" or a "holy man,"[80] Nietzsche offered his concept of Dionysus as a new "faith" to replace Christian faith or, at a minimum, as a semi-religious philosophical substitute for Christianity. He summarized this offer at the very end of *Ecce Homo* with the words: "Have I been understood? – *Dionysus versus the Crucified*."[81] His concept of Dionysus symbolizes the affirmation of life in its totality, saying Yes to all aspects of life, and the joy of becoming as well as the joy in destruction, which he presented in contrast to the Christian negation of life, denial of reality, and corruption of humanity.

In *Twilight of the Idols*, Nietzsche explained the ancient Greek concept of Dionysus and why he chose this name to represent his own concept.

118

For it is only in the Dionysian mysteries, in the psychology of the Dionysian condition, that the *fundamental fact* of the Hellenic instinct expresses itself – its "will to life." *What* did the Hellene guarantee to himself with these mysteries? *Eternal* life, the eternal recurrence of life; the future promised and consecrated in the past; the triumphant Yes to life beyond death and change; *true* life as collective continuation of life through procreation, through the mysteries of sexuality. It was for this reason that the *sexual* symbol was to the Greeks the symbol venerable as such, the intrinsic profound meaning of all antique piety. Every individual detail in the act of pro-creation, pregnancy, birth, awoke the most exalted and solemn feelings. In the teachings of the mysteries, *pain* is sanctified: the "pains of childbirth" sanctify pain in general – all becoming and growing, all that guarantees the future, *postulates* pain. . . . For the eternal joy in creating to exist, for the will to life eternally to affirm itself, the "torment of childbirth" *must* also exist eternally. . . . All this is contained in the word Dionysus: I know of no more exalted symbolism than this *Greek* symbolism, the symbolism of the Dionysian. The profoundest instinct of life, the instinct for the future of life, for the eternity of life, is in this word experienced religiously – the actual road to life, procreation, as the *sacred road.* . . . It was only Christianity, with *ressentiment against* life in its foundations, which made of sexuality something impure: it threw *filth* on the beginning, on the prerequisite of our life . . .[82]

Unlike his concept of Dionysus in *The Birth of Tragedy* (1872) where Nietzsche contrasted the Dionysian with the Apollinian, his concept of Dionysus in all his books and notes after *Zarathustra* (1883-1885) symbolized the affirmation of life in contrast to the Christian negation of life. Christianity "is nihilistic in the most profound sense, while in the Dionysian symbol the ultimate limit of affirmation is attained."[83] The Dionysian "*affirms* all that is questionable and terrible in existence."[84] "Affirmation of life even in its strangest and sternest problems, the will to life rejoicing in its own inexhaustibility through the *sacrifice* of its highest types – *that* is what I called Dionysian."[85]

In *Ecce Homo*, Nietzsche elaborated on the opposition between the Dionysian and the "Crucified." In the section on *The Birth of Tragedy*, Nietzsche claimed that he was

> the first to see the real opposition: the degenerating instinct that turns against life with subterranean vengefulness (Christianity, the philosophy of Schopenhauer, in a certain sense already the philosophy of Plato, and all of idealism as typical forms) versus a formula for the highest affirmation, born of fullness, of overfullness, a Yes-saying without reservation, even to suffering, even to guilt, even to everything that is questionable and strange in existence.
>
> This ultimate, most joyous, most wantonly extravagant Yes to life represents not only the highest insight but also the *deepest*, that which is most strictly confirmed and born out by truth and science. Nothing in existence may be subtracted, nothing is dispensable. [. . .]
>   [. . .]
> Whoever does not merely comprehend the word "Dionysian" but comprehends *himself* in the word "Dionysian" needs no refutation of Plato or Christianity or Schopenhauer – he *smells the decay*.[86]

In retrospect, Nietzsche wrote that it was his instinct that turned against Christian morality in *The Birth of Tragedy* and that discovered "a fundamentally opposite doctrine and valuation of life – purely artistic and *anti-Christian*," which he "baptized [. . .] in the name of a Greek god: I called it Dionysian."[87]

In his notes of 1888, Nietzsche further explained this "antithesis" of "Dionysus versus the 'Crucified.'" It is a difference in the meaning of their martyrdom. For Dionysus, "life itself, its eternal fruitfulness and recurrence, creates torment, destruction, the will to annihilation." For the "Crucified," "suffering [. . .] counts as an objection to this life, as a formula for its condemnation." The problem is the meaning of suffering. With a tragic or Dionysian meaning, "being is counted as *holy enough* to justify even a monstrous amount of suffering. The tragic man affirms even the harshest suffering: he is sufficiently strong, rich, and capable of deifying to do so." With a Christian meaning,

> it is supposed to be the path to a holy existence [. . .] The Christian denies even the happiest lot on earth: he is sufficiently weak, poor, disinherited to suffer from life in whatever form he meets it. The god on the cross is a curse on life, a signpost to seek redemption from life; Dionysus cut to pieces is a *promise* of life: it will be eternally reborn and return again from destruction.[88]

As an historical example, Nietzsche asserted that Johann Wolfgang von Goethe – "the last German before whom I feel reverence"[89] – represented the Dionysian faith.

> What he [i.e., Goethe] aspired to was *totality*; he strove against the separation of reason, sensuality, feeling, will [. . .]; he disciplined himself to a whole, he *created* himself. [. . .] Goethe conceived of a strong, highly cultured human being, skilled in all physical accomplishments, who, keeping himself in check and having reverence for himself, dares to allow himself the whole compass and wealth of naturalness, who is strong enough for this freedom; a man of tolerance, not out of weakness, but out of strength, because he knows how to employ to his advantage what would destroy an average nature; a man to whom nothing is forbidden, except it be *weakness*, whether that weakness be called vice or virtue. . . . A spirit thus *emancipated* stands in the midst of the universe with a joyful and trusting fatalism, in the *faith* that only what is separate and individual may be rejected, that in the totality everything is redeemed and affirmed – *he no longer denies*. . . . But such a faith is the highest of all possible faiths: I have baptized it with the name *Dionysus*.[90]

This "highest of all possible faiths" is the faith that allows one to will the eternal recurrence of all things.[91]

This Dionysian "faith" that "nothing is dispensable," that "in the totality everything is redeemed and affirmed," includes the "affirmation of passing away *and destroying*, which is the decisive feature of a Dionysian philosophy; saying Yes to opposition and war; *becoming*, along with a radical repudiation of the very concept of *being*."[92]

> He that is richest in the fullness of life, the Dionysian god and man, cannot only afford the sight of the terrible and questionable but even the terrible deed and any luxury of destruction, decomposition, and negation. In his case, what is evil, absurd, and ugly seems, as it were, permissible, owing to an excess of procreating, fertilizing energies that can still turn any desert into lush farmland.[93]

The Dionysian man creates in order "*to realize in oneself* the eternal joy of becoming – that joy which also encompasses *joy in destruction*."[94] Although the "desire for *destruction*, change, and becoming can be an expression of an overflowing energy that is pregnant with future (my term for this is, as is known, 'Dionysian')," Nietzsche warned that "it can also be the hatred of the ill-constituted, disinherited, and under-privileged, who destroy, *must* destroy, because what exists, indeed all existence, all being, outrages and provokes them."[95] Only when the destruction is accompanied by creation is it Dionysian. "We can destroy only as creators."[96] For Nietzsche, destruction is always a prelude to construction.[97]

Before continuing the discussion of this dual theme of destruction and creation in the next chapter, we shall revisit the topic of the philosophers of the future.

G. Philosophers of the Future Redux

As discussed earlier,[98] Nietzsche assigned to the philosophers of the future the tasks of completing the philosophy of the future and of establishing a new nobility to tackle the task of the higher breeding of humanity. These philosophers of the future also have a role to play in the religion of the future. They will use this new religion – the Dionysian faith – in their project of human enhancement.

After only two chapters on philosophy, the next chapter in *Beyond Good and Evil* is on religion in which Nietzsche showed how the "religion of the future arises naturally out of the philosophy of the future."[99] In one of the most important sections of the book, he alluded to the idea of the eternal recurrence in describing the crucial insight of this new religion. This insight appears as a new ideal glimpsed as a result of thinking pessimism – "the most world-denying of all possible ways of thinking" – through to its depths – "beyond good and evil and no longer [. . .] under the spell and delusion of morality" – in order to see "the opposite ideal" of this world-denying pessimism. This new "opposite" ideal is "the ideal of the most high-spirited, alive, and world-affirming human being who has not only come to terms and learned to get along with whatever was and is, but who wants to have *what was and is* repeated into all eternity, shouting insatiably *da capo* ["from the beginning"]."[100] This new ideal, of course, is the Overman as represented by Zarathustra, the one "with an Asiatic and supra-Asiatic eye,"[101] who attains redemption through the willing of the eternal recurrence of all things.[102] In *Beyond Good and Evil*, this ideal is embodied in the philosopher of the future.

This Dionysian ideal is linked to an earlier section in the same chapter in which Nietzsche praised the religiosity of the ancient Greeks because of "the enormous abundance of gratitude it exudes: it is a very noble type of man that confronts nature and life in *this* way."[103] This new appreciation of religion prepares the reader for the return of Dionysus and Ariadne at the end of the book.[104] As the embodiment of the new Dionysian ideal, the noble philosopher of the future will share this religious outlook toward "nature and life"[105] and will substitute a religion of gratitude for the Christian one of faith through the idea of the eternal recurrence.[106]

The philosophers of the future will use their Dionysian faith – the idea of the eternal recurrence – in their project of human enhancement. Knowing "what religions are good for"[107] and with the whole development of humanity on his conscience, the philosopher of the future

> will make use of religions for his project of breeding and education [*Züchtungs- und Erziehungswerke*] [. . .] The selective and cultivating [*züchtende*] influence, always destructive as well as

creative and form-giving, which can be exerted with the help of religions, is always multiple and different according to the sort of human beings who are placed under its spell and protection.[108]

In short, religions should "be a means of breeding and education [Züchtungs- und Erziehungsmittel] in the philosopher's hand."[109]

It is no accident that Nietzsche ventured to "baptize" the philosophers of the future with the name "*attempters*" [*Versucher*][110] and also called Dionysus the "tempter god" [*Versucher-Gott*].[111] The primary meaning of *Versucher* is an experimenter, which is consistent with the experimental nature of the "project of breeding and education," that is, the project of human enhancement. Dionysus, as the *Versucher-Gott*, can then be best understood as the god of the experimenters.

Perhaps as part of his own experiment in god creation, Nietzsche had Dionysus in mind when he lamented in *The Anti-Christ* that "the strong races of northern Europe have not repudiated the Christian God" nor

> felt *compelled* to have done with such a sickly and decrepit product of *décadence*. But there lies a curse on them for not having had done with it: they have taken up sickness, old age, contradiction into all their instincts – since then they have failed to *create* a God! Almost two millennia and not a single new God![112]

More concretely, Nietzsche provided four ways in which the Dionysian faith could be used by the philosophers of the future in their experimental project of human enhancement. One way is to replace the Christian ascetic ideal, "an ideal of decadence," with a counter ideal, the idea of the eternal recurrence. Although the ascetic ideal was "the *harmful* ideal *par excellence*, [. . .] it was the only ideal so far, because it had no rival. 'For man would rather will even nothingness than *not* will.' – Above all, a *counterideal* was lacking – *until Zarathustra*."[113] Zarathustra's doctrine of the eternal recurrence is the new counter ideal that can now be willed by humanity.

Second, the idea of the eternal recurrence provides the criterion for fitness to rule in the new aristocratic society that Nietzsche envisaged. In his description of this society in *The Anti-Christ*, he explained that the "highest caste" – "the predominately spiritual type" – is the "perfect caste" that has "the most spiritual, the affirmative instinct" that speaks: "*The world is perfect.*" These "most spiritual human beings" are "the *strongest.*"[114] Finding the world "perfect" is the result of the willing of the eternal recurrence of all things. Only those higher types who have willed the eternal recurrence of all things are fit to rule. Recall that Zarathustra's world became perfect after his redemption.[115]

In his notes, Nietzsche revealed that the third way that the idea of the eternal recurrence could be used in the project of human enhancement is as a breeding idea or agent. In one note, he wrote that one of his fundamental innovations is to replace "metaphysics" and religion with "the theory of eternal recurrence (this as a means of breeding [*Züchtung*] and selection [*Auswahl*])."[116] This note also supports the argument that the idea of the eternal recurrence – the Dionysian faith – was intended to replace contemporary religion.

Referring to the doctrine of the eternal recurrence, Nietzsche also wrote, "A doctrine is needed powerful enough to work as a breeding [*züchtend*] agent; strengthening the strong, paralyzing and destructive for the world-weary."[117] In other words, if "this thought [of eternal recurrence] gained possession of you, it would change you as you are or perhaps crush you"[118] if you are not strong enough for it. The idea of the eternal recurrence allows those who ought to perish to perish, namely, those who cannot bear the eternal recurrence of all things. In *Zarathustra*, this idea demonstrates its breeding or cultivating function by crushing "the spirit of gravity that moves all teachers of revenge" and by exhilarating "the opposite spirit of affirmation."[119]

The stimulus of the demon[120] to our will to power to act in such a way that we become well enough disposed to ourselves and to life to crave nothing more fervently than this eternal recurrence is perhaps what Nietzsche meant when he wrote that his "philosophy brings the triumphant idea of which all other modes of thought will ultimately perish. It is the great cultivating idea [*der grosse züchtende Gedanke*]: the races that cannot bear it stand condemned; those who find it the greatest benefit are chosen to rule."[121]

Finally, *Zarathustra* can serve as the primary religious work of the Dionysian faith. As we have seen,[122] the idea of the eternal recurrence is the "fundamental conception" and "basic idea"[123] of *Zarathustra* as well as the "doctrine of Zarathustra."[124] In his notes, Nietzsche referred to *Zarathustra* as "a fifth Gospel" and a "new 'holy book'" that "challenges all existing religions."[125] He intended this "profoundest book" that humanity possesses[126] to be the central, sacred text of the new religion that is to replace Christianity.[127]

As the basis of both the philosophy of the future and the religion of the future, the idea of the eternal recurrence is the foundational idea of a new era. As "the teacher of the eternal recurrence,"[128] Nietzsche deemed it his destiny to be the herald of this new era.

---

[1] TI IX, §49.

[2] EH-BT, §4. Nietzsche called the ancient Greeks "the *supreme cultural event* of history." TI IX, §47.

[3] BT, Attempt at a Self-Criticism, §1.

[4] BT, §20.

[5] "Let no one try to blight our faith in a yet-impending rebirth of Hellenic antiquity; for this alone gives us hope for a renovation and purification of the German spirit through the fire magic of music." Ibid.

[6] Young, *Nietzsche*, 360. Young suggests that "Nietzsche's whole life and philosophy is, above all else, a struggle to find a new religious outlook that will re-found 'culture.'" Ibid., 181.

[7] EH-BT, §4. In 1876, Nietzsche recognized "in Wagner such a counter-Alexander." UM IV, §4.

[8] EH-BT, §4. This Great Noon is the same as that discussed in chap. 3 above.

[9] Recall Zarathustra's victory over the "spirit of gravity" and Platonism. See chap. 4, sect. F, above.

[10] Lampert, *Nietzsche's Task*, 288.

[11] Lampert, *Nietzsche's Teaching*, 227.

[12] Ibid., 231.

[13] Z III, On the Great Longing.

[14] Z III, The Other Dancing Song, §1.

[15] Lampert, *Nietzsche's Teaching*, 227.

[16] Ibid., 235.

[17] GS, §342.

[18] EH-Z, §1.

[19] EH-BT, §4.

[20] Nietzsche's concept of the Dionysian in *The Birth of Tragedy*, where he contrasted it with the Apollinian, is very different from his concept of the Dionysian after

Zarathustra. See chap. 6, sect. F, below.

21 BGE, §295.

22 See chap. 4, sect. E, above.

23 EH-Z, §6.

24 Nietzsche called Zarathustra a "Dionysian monster." BT, Attempt at a Self-Criticism, §7.

25 EH-Z, §6.

26 EH-Z, §1.

27 EH-Z, §6.

28 Z III, On Old and New Tablets, §19.

29 EH-Z, §6 (quoting Z III, On Old and New Tablets, §19).

30 EH-Z, §6.

31 Ibid.

32 Ibid.

33 EH-BT, §3.

34 The last outline of the planned four-volume *Revaluation of All Values* had Book IV entitled "Dionysus. Philosophy of the Eternal Return." Young, *Nietzsche*, 542.

35 NW, Epilogue, §1.

36 Although Nietzsche defined his task as the same as Zarathustra's, which was to say "Yes to the point of justifying, of redeeming even all of the past," and then quoted a passage from *Zarathustra* defining redemption, EH-Z, §8 (see chap. 4, sect. B, above), he never wrote that he was "redeemed."

37 EH II, §10.

38 EH-BT, §2.

39 WP, §1041.

40 GS, §276. In the next section, Nietzsche wrote about "the idea of a personal providence" that allows us to "see how palpably always everything that happens to us turns out for the best." GS, §277.

41 EH I, §6.

42 WLN, 7[38]. Nietzsche expressed the same idea more poetically in Z IV, The Drunken Song, §10.

43 See chap. 4, sect. E, above.

44 GM III, §14. Recall that Zarathustra overcame his nausea at humanity in the first three parts of *Zarathustra* and overcame his pity for humanity in the fourth part. See chap. 4, sects. A through D, above.

45 EH I, §8.

46 EH IV, §6.

47 EH, Preface. Compare to Zarathustra's experience of the perfection of the world after his redemption. Z IV, At Noon.

48 EH, Preface.

49 Walter Kaufman, introduction to Nietzsche, *On the Genealogy of Morals* and *Ecce Homo*, 206-7. This attitude of gratitude is expressed well in one of Nietzsche's best known maxims: "What does not kill me makes me stronger." TI I, §8.

50 EH I, §6. "For a typically healthy person, conversely, being sick can even become an energetic *stimulus* for life, for living *more*. This, in fact, is how that long period of

sickness appears to me *now*: as it were, I discovered life anew, including myself; I tasted all good and even little things, as others cannot easily taste them – I turned my will to health, to *life*, into a philosophy." EH I, §2.

[51] EH II, §9.

[52] EH II, §10.

[53] EH-CW, §4.

[54] NW, Epilogue, §1.

[55] See chap. 4, sect. B, above.

[56] EH-Z, §8.

[57] BGE, §295.

[58] BT, Attempt at a Self-Criticism, §4.

[59] TI X, §5.

[60] EH, Preface, §2. In Greek mythology, satyrs were the male companions of Dionysus.

[61] EH III, §6.

[62] R. J. Hollingdale, introduction to Friedrich Nietzsche, *Dithyrambs of Dionysus*, trans. R. J. Hollingdale (London: Anvil Press Poetry, 2001), 11.

[63] Ibid., 16.

[64] EH-Z, §6, is discussed in chap. 6, sect. B, above.

[65] EH-Z, §7.

[66] EH-Z, §8.

[67] "As 1888 turned into 1889, then, Nietzsche, in a confused way, 'becomes' the god Dionysus." Young, *Nietzsche*, 530.

[68] Cate, *Nietzsche*, 549; Nietzsche, *Selected Letters*, 345-46.

[69] Nietzsche, *Selected Letters*, 346.

[70] BT, Attempt at a Self-Criticism, §5.

[71] EH IV, §9. See chap. 6, sect. F, below.

[72] EH-GM. If read in context, Nietzsche could have been referring to himself as Dionysus in this quotation.

[73] A, §62. "I *condemn* Christianity [. . .] I call Christianity the *one* great curse, the *one* great intrinsic depravity, the *one* great instinct for revenge for which no expedient is sufficiently poisonous, secret, subterranean, *petty* – I call it the *one* immortal blemish of mankind." Ibid.

[74] Friedrich Nietzsche, *The Anti-Christ, Ecce Homo, Twilight of the Idols And Other Writings*, ed. Aaron Ridley and Judith Norman (Cambridge: Cambridge University Press, 2005), 66-67. Hollingdale's translation does not include the "Law against Christianity."

[75] Z IV, The Awakening, §2; Z IV, The Ass Festival.

[76] EH III, §2.

[77] Nietzsche, *Selected Letters*, 211.

[78] Ibid., 219.

[79] BGE, §256.

[80] EH IV, §1. "Religions are affairs of the rabble." Ibid.

[81] EH IV, §9.

[82] TI X, §4.

83 EH-BT, §1.
84 TI III, §6.
85 TI X, §5.
86 EH-BT, §2.
87 BT, Attempt at a Self-Criticism, §5.
88 WP, §1052.
89 TI IX, §51. Nietzsche and Goethe were "in agreement over the 'Cross.'" Ibid.
90 TI IX, §49.
91 Young, *Nietzsche*, 501.
92 EH-BT, §3.
93 GS, §370.
94 TI X, §5.
95 GS, §370.
96 GS, §58.
97 Young, *Nietzsche*, 247.
98 See chap. 5, sect. F, above.
99 Lampert, *Nietzsche's Task*, 114.
100 BGE, §56.
101 Ibid.
102 Lampert, *Nietzsche's Task*, 117-18.
103 BGE, §49.
104 Lampert, *Nietzsche's Task*, 101.
105 Douglas Burnham, *Reading Nietzsche: An Analysis of "Beyond Good and Evil"* (Montreal: McGill-Queen's University Press, 2007), 79.
106 Ibid., 89-90. In *The Anti-Christ*, Nietzsche contrasted the Christian concept of god with that of an earlier time when the gods expressed "the will to power" and religion was "a form of gratitude." A, §16.
107 BGE, §58.
108 BGE, §61. Kaufmann's translation of *Züchtung* has been changed from "cultivation" to "breeding."
109 BGE, §62. Kaufmann's translation of *Züchtung* has been changed from "cultivation" to "breeding."
110 BGE, §42. In predicting and calling for the appearance of "philosophers of the future," Nietzsche ventured to "baptize" them with the name "*attempters* [*Versucher*]. This name itself is in the end a mere attempt [*Versuch*] and, if you will, a temptation [*Versuchung*]." Ibid. The term *Versucher* can be understood in four different ways. The first is as an "experimenter." Later, Nietzsche wrote that the philosophers of the future will certainly be "men of experiments [*Experimente*]." BGE, §210. In addition to "attempt," *Versuch* also means a scientific experiment. *Langenscheidt*, s.v. "Versuch." For this reason, experimenter may be considered Nietzsche's primary meaning of *Versucher*. Experimenter is also consistent with the second way in which *Versucher* may be understood. That second way is as an "attempter," which implies possible failure of an attempt or experiment and which corresponds with his comment that the name is "in the end a mere attempt." The third is as a "tempter," which corresponds with Nietzsche's comment that the name is "a temptation."

Finally, the fourth way in which *Versucher* can be understood is as an essayist or essayer whose mode of expression is the essay or aphorism. *Versuch* is the German translation of "essay." Lampert, *Nietzsche's Task*, 95-96.

[111] BGE, §295.

[112] A, §19. In a note intended to be Section 20 of *The Anti-Christ*, Nietzsche wrote, "– And how many new gods are still possible! As for myself, in whom the religious, that is to say god-forming, instinct occasionally becomes active at impossible times – how differently, how variously the divine has revealed itself to me each time!" WP, §1038.

[113] EH-GM.

[114] A, §57. "Being able to will the eternal return as the condition of becoming a leader of Nietzsche's ideal community turns out to provide the apex of his political philosophy." Young, *Friedrich Nietzsche*, 542.

[115] Z IV, At Noon. Also, recall that Nietzsche began *Ecce Homo* on "this perfect day," his forty-fourth birthday. EH, Preface.

[116] WP, §462.

[117] WP, §862.

[118] GS, §341.

[119] Lampert, *Nietzsche's Task*, 135-36.

[120] GS, §341. See chap. 4, sect. F, above.

[121] WP, §1053.

[122] See chap. 4, sect. F, above.

[123] EH-Z, §1.

[124] EH-BT, §3.

[125] Young, *Nietzsche*, 366.

[126] TI IX, §51. "To create things upon which time tries its teeth in vain; in form and in *substance* to strive after a little immortality – I have never been modest enough to demand less of myself. [. . .] I have given mankind the profoundest book it possesses, my *Zarathustra*: I shall shortly give it the most independent [i.e., *The Anti-Christ*]." Ibid.

[127] Young, *Nietzsche*, 366. After hearing in July 1883 from his anti-Semitic publisher that none of the printed copies of *Zarathustra* had yet left the printer's workshop because of other printing priorities of his publisher, Nietzsche complained to a friend in a letter, "It is truly laughable: first of all the Christian obstacle, the 500,000 hymnals, and now the Jew-hating obstacle – these are altogether 'experiences of the founders of religion.'" In other words, he was now personally experiencing the hostility that all great religious reformers experience. Cate, *Nietzsche*, 399.

[128] TI X, §5.

Chapter 7

DESTINY

Nietzsche explained in the last chapter of *Ecce Homo* entitled "Why I Am a Destiny" that his uncovering of Christian morality – a part of his revaluation of all values – was what defined him and set him apart from the whole rest of humanity.[1] That is the reason he claimed to be "a destiny." "The uncovering of Christian morality is an event without parallel, a real catastrophe. He that is enlightened about that, is a *force majeure* ["superior force"], a destiny – he breaks the history of mankind in two. One lives before him, or one lives after him."[2] Concerning the time after him, Nietzsche declared that "it is only beginning with me that there are hopes again, tasks, ways that can be prescribed for culture – *I am he that brings these glad tidings.* – And thus I am also a destiny."[3]

Nietzsche made the same claim about breaking history into two halves in his private letters. In referring to *The Anti-Christ* in a letter to a friend, dated 14 September 1888, Nietzsche wrote,

> In the last analysis, both these works [*Case of Wagner* and *Twilight of the Idols*] are only recuperations in the midst of an immeasurably difficult and decisive task which, *when it is understood*, will split humanity into two halves. Its aim and meaning is, in four words: the *transvaluation of all values.* [. . .] To be a Christian – one consequence among others – will be hereafter *improper.* Much is already astir in this most radical revolution that mankind has known.[4]

Nietzsche had already set the date for this breaking of human history into two halves in *The Anti-Christ*. This book was initially intended to be the first of four parts of a book to be entitled *Revaluation of All Values*[5] but then became the only part.[6] As already noted,[7] he rhetorically asked at the end of that book why not calculate time from the last day of Christianity – from the day he completed *The Anti-Christ* on 30 September 1888.[8] He then ended the book with the words: "Revaluation of all values!"[9]

Nietzsche realized that his revaluation of all values would create a crisis on earth.

> I know my fate. One day my name will be associated with the memory of something tremendous – a crisis without equal on earth, the most profound collision of conscience, a decision that was conjured up *against* everything that had been believed, demanded, hallowed so far. I am no man, I am dynamite.[10]

Despite the predictions of calamity, Nietzsche did not perceive this crisis as wholly negative.

> I contradict as has never been contradicted before and am nevertheless the opposite of a No-saying spirit. I am a bringer of glad tidings like no one before me; I know tasks of such elevation that any notion of them has been lacking so far; only beginning with me are there hopes again. For all that, I am necessarily also the man of calamity. For when truth enters into a fight with the lies of millennia, we shall have upheavals, a convulsion of earthquakes, a moving of mountains and valleys, the like of which has never been dreamed of. The concept of politics will have merged entirely with a war of spirits; all power structures of the old society will have been exploded – all of them are based on lies: there will be wars the like of which have never yet been seen on earth. It is only beginning with me that the earth knows *great politics*.[11]

Nietzsche accepted this coming crisis and his role in it as necessary. He realized that the greatest creative acts are preceded by acts of destruction. To create the new, one must first destroy the old.

> You want a formula for such a destiny *become man?* That is to be found in my *Zarathustra*:
>
> "And whoever wants to be a creator in good and evil, must first be an annihilator and break values. Thus the highest evil belongs to the greatest goodness: but this is — being creative."
>
> I am by far the most terrible human being that has existed so far; this does not preclude the possibility that I shall be the most beneficial. I know the pleasure in destroying to a degree that accords with my powers to destroy — in both respects I obey my Dionysian nature which does not know how to separate doing No from saying Yes. I am the first immoralist: that makes me the annihilator *par excellence*.[12]

In other words, Nietzsche declared, "If a temple [*Heiligtum*] is to be erected *a temple must be destroyed*: that is the law — let anyone who can show me a case in which it is not fulfilled!"[13] Recognizing that he was only the herald and precursor of "better players,"[14] Nietzsche looked to the future for the redeeming "creative spirit" who will be strong and healthy enough to attain the goal of destroying the temple of Christianity and its slave morality and erecting a new temple or religion in its place.[15]

> The attainment of this goal would require a *different* kind of spirit from that likely to appear in this present age: spirits strengthened by war and victory, for whom conquest, adventure, danger, and even pain have become needs; it would require habituation to the keen air of the heights, to winter journeys, to ice and mountains in every sense; it would require even a kind of sublime wickedness, an ultimate, supremely self-confident mischievousness in knowledge that goes with great health; it would require, in brief and alas, precisely this *great health!*

Is this even possible today? – But some day, in a stronger age than this decaying, self-doubting present, he must yet come to us, the *redeeming* man of great love and contempt, the creative spirit whose compelling strength will not let him rest in any aloofness or any beyond, whose isolation is misunderstood by the people as if it were flight *from* reality – while it is only his absorption, immersion, penetration *into* reality, so that, when he one day emerges again into the light, he may bring home the *redemption* of this reality: its redemption from the curse that the hitherto reigning ideal has laid upon it. This man of the future, who will redeem us not only from the hitherto reigning ideal but also from that which was bound to grow out of it, the great nausea, the will to nothingness, nihilism; this bell-stroke of noon and of the great decision that liberates the will again and restores its goal to the earth and his hope to man; this Antichrist and antinihilist; this victor over God and nothingness – *he must come one day.* –[16]

In the next section, Nietzsche stopped himself from writing anymore on this subject unless he usurped that "to which only *Zarathustra* has a right, *Zarathustra the godless.* –"[17] The connection between this redeeming "man of the future" and Zarathustra can be found in the type of man that Zarathustra wants. Like the "man of the future," Zarathustra's type of man penetrates reality.

It is here and nowhere else that one must make a start to comprehend what Zarathustra wants: this type of man that he conceives, conceives reality *as it is*, being strong enough to do so; this type is not estranged or removed from reality but is reality itself and exemplifies all that is terrible and questionable in it – *only in that way can man attain greatness.*[18]

As mentioned earlier,[19] Nietzsche's formula for greatness in a human being is *amor fati*,[20] which was his personal expression for the willing of the eternal recurrence of all things. Conceiving reality as it is and being reality itself are consequences of willing the eternal recurrence of all things, as are the absorption, immersion, and penetration into reality. By willing the eternal recurrence of all things, both the redeeming "man of the future" and Zarathustra's type of man have attained redemption and thereby have become the Overman. That is the reason only Zarathustra, who, as the Overman, has "the hardest, most terrible insight into reality, that has thought the 'most abysmal idea' [i.e., the idea of the eternal recurrence],"[21] has a right to write anymore on the "man of the future."

Like Zarathustra, this "creative spirit," this "man of the future," will redeem us from "the hitherto reigning ideal" (i.e., the "spirit of gravity" or Platonism, Christianity, and the democratic enlightenment) as well as the "nihilism" that was bound to grow out of it. This event occurs at the "bell-stroke of noon" when "the great decision" is made "that liberates the will again and restores its goal to the earth and his hope to man."[22] In other words, this event is the Great Noon (i.e., the "bell-stroke of noon") when the questions of Why? and For What? are answered and those answers (i.e., "the great decision") are faithful both to the earth (i.e., the higher breeding of humanity) and to humanity (i.e., the enhancement of humanity), thereby restoring "its goal to the earth and his hope to man."[23]

The event of the Great Noon includes the "return of the Greek spirit."[24] As we have seen,[25] the "Greek spirit" that Nietzsche wanted to see return is embodied in his concept of the Dionysian. He transposed the Dionysian into a "philosophical pathos" and called it "*tragic wisdom.*" He also called himself "the first *tragic philosopher.*"[26]

In the second edition of *The Gay Science* (1887), Nietzsche called this tragic wisdom by another name. He called it Dionysian pessimism. In opposition to the "*romantic pessimism*" of Arthur Schopenhauer and Richard Wagner, Nietzsche saw coming a different kind of pessimism that is associated with "the *over-fullness of life*" that wants "a Dionysian art and likewise a tragic view of life, a tragic insight." "I call this pessimism of the future – for it comes! I see it coming! – *Dionysian* pessimism."[27]

Using the word "tragic" in the same Dionysian sense, Nietzsche promised a "tragic age" in which he hoped for "a Dionysian future of music."

Let us look ahead a century; let us suppose that my attempt to assassinate two millennia of antinature and desecration of man [i.e., the revaluation of all values] were to succeed. That new party of life which would tackle the greatest of all tasks, the higher breeding of humanity, including the relentless destruction of everything that was degenerating and parasitical, would again make possible that excess of life on earth from which the Dionysian state, too, would have to arise again. I promise a tragic age: the highest art in saying Yes to life, tragedy, will be reborn when humanity has weathered the consciousness of the hardest but most necessary wars *without suffering from it*.[28]

This tragic age – the golden age of the new era – will arise only after the new era has commenced and the new nobility has begun to tackle the task of the higher breeding of humanity. The rebirth of tragedy also requires the weathering "of the hardest but most necessary wars *without suffering from it*."[29] Nietzsche realized, however, that the Great Noon, inaugurating the new era, was also, like the tragic age, still far in the future.

---

[1] EH IV, §7.

[2] EH IV, §8.

[3] EH-TI, §2.

[4] Nietzsche, *Selected Letters*, 311. *Die Umwertung aller Werte* is sometimes translated as "transvaluation of all values" instead of "revaluation of all values."

[5] TI, Foreword.

[6] EH-TI, §3; Young, *Nietzsche*, 541.

[7] See cited text at n. 32 on p. 35 above.

[8] TI, Foreword.

[9] A, §62.

[10] EH IV, §1.

[11] Ibid.

[12] EH IV, §2 (quoting Z II, On Self-Overcoming).

[13] GM II, §24.

[14] Z III, On Old and New Tablets, §20.

[15] Since *Heiligtum* ("temple" or "shrine") is a religious term, the implication is that Christianity will not be replaced by atheism but by an alternative religious philosophy or faith.

[16] GM II, §24.

[17] GM II, §25.

[18] EH IV, §5.

[19] See chap. 6, sect. C, above.

[20] EH II, §10.

[21] EH-Z, §6.

[22] GM II, §24.

[23] See the end of chap. 3 above.

[24] EH-BT, §4.

[25] See chap. 6, sect. A, above.

[26] EH-BT, §3.

[27] GS, §370. This "premonition and vision belongs to me as inseparable from me, as my *proprium* and *ipsissimum* ["my own and my quintessence"]." Ibid.

[28] EH-BT, §4. Kaufmann's translation of "*die Höherzüchtung der Menschheit*" has been modified. See n. 39 on p. 37 above. Also, the word "awaken" at the end of the second sentence has been changed to "arise." The original German word is *erwachsen* ("to arise" or "develop") and not *erwachen* ("to awake"). Friedrich Nietzsche, *Sämtliche Werke: Kritische Studienausgabe*, ed. Giorgio Colli and Mazzino Montinari (Munich: de Gruyter, 1999), 6:313.

[29] EH-BT, §4.

CONCLUSION

Nietzsche realized that his time had not yet come. In the foreword to *The Anti-Christ*, he wrote, "Only the day after tomorrow belongs to me. Some are born posthumously."[1] With our new understanding of the significance of his philosophy to us, may we now dare say that Nietzsche has been reborn?

Nietzsche thought that most people do not comprehend contemporary greatness, whether of events, thoughts, or individuals. "The greatest events and thoughts – but the greatest thoughts are the greatest events – are comprehended last: the generations that are contemporaneous with them do not *experience* such events – they live right past them."[2] While the greatest thoughts are the greatest events, the greatest thoughts are the creation of new values. In his speech on the flies of the market place, Zarathustra says little "do the people comprehend the great – that is, the creating." "Around the inventors of new values the world revolves: invisibly it revolves. But around the actors revolve the people and fame: that is 'the way of the world.'"[3]

Nietzsche was an inventor of new values or, as he expressed it elsewhere, a new "teacher of the purpose of existence." In the first section of *The Gay Science*, he wrote that the ever new appearance in history of teachers of the purpose of existence (e.g., "founders of moralities and religions") has changed human nature and has created

> the need for the ever new appearance of such teachers and teachings of a "purpose."
>
> Gradually, man has become a fantastic animal that has to fulfill one more condition of existence than any other animal: man *has to* believe, to know, from time to time *why* he

exists; his race cannot flourish without a periodic trust in life
– without faith in *reason in life*.[4]

Because of this "new law of ebb and flood," Nietzsche announced, "There is a time for us, too!"[5] In other words, because of the
death of the Christian god that he will proclaim later in the same book,
there will be a time for a new "teacher of the purpose of existence."
Nietzsche is that teacher for the new era.

Nietzsche called the nineteenth-century European cultural event
in which the belief in the Christian god has become unbelievable by
the provocative expression "God is dead." This event was the death
knell of the old era. Instead of waiting for Christian morality to collapse
and perish as he predicted would happen as a result of the death of the
Christian god, Nietzsche condemned Christianity and wanted to
"crush the infamy"[6] because the anti-natural slave morality of Christianity is "the extremist thinkable form of corruption."[7]

According to Nietzsche, there are two kinds of morality – master
or noble morality ("Roman," "pagan," "classical," "Renaissance") and
slave or *ressentiment* morality (Judaism, Christianity). He symbolized the
centuries-long struggle between these two antithetical kinds with the
expression, "Rome against Judea, Judea against Rome."[8] Heretofore,
Judea has been victorious over Rome. This victory has been reinforced
by the democratic movement, the heir of Christianity.

In response to the victory of slave morality and the consequent
continued corruption of humanity, Nietzsche considered his life's task
to be a revaluation of all values. This means a new evaluation of all the
ressentiment or slave values of Christian morality. Such a revaluation is
the prerequisite for the creation of a new master morality.

Nietzsche's task of a revaluation of all values may be divided into
two aspects: a personal and a public. In turn, the personal aspect may
be divided between the Yes-saying part and the No-saying, No-doing
part. The Yes-saying part culminated in the idea of the eternal recurrence – the basis of both the philosophy of the future and the religion
of the future. The No-saying, No-doing part was intended to rekindle
the struggle between master morality and slave morality and to ultimately lead to the victory of a new master morality.

Nietzsche wanted the victory of master morality. He linked the "salvation and future of the human race with the unconditional dominance"[9] of master morality and called master morality "a higher order of values, the noble ones, those that say Yes to life, those that guarantee the future."[10] Just as "there is an order of rank between man and man," there is also an order of rank "between morality and morality."[11]

Both parts of the personal aspect of Nietzsche's task were in preparation for a moment of the highest self-contemplation of humanity, which he called the Great Noon. This event is the public aspect of Nietzsche's task at which the most elect, a new party of life, consecrate themselves to the greatest of all tasks, the higher breeding of humanity, with the goal of human enhancement. The Great Noon inaugurates the new era.

Nietzsche made preparations for the Great Noon with both *Thus Spoke Zarathustra* and *Beyond Good and Evil*, although each in a "very different" way. In a letter to his friend, the famous historian Jakob Burckhardt, dated 22 September 1886, Nietzsche wrote that *Beyond Good and Evil* "says the same things as my *Zarathustra* – only in a way that is different – very different."[12] Both books begin with a choice between continuing the current course of history toward the "last man" on the one hand and following, and further developing and completing, Nietzsche's philosophy of the future toward the creation of higher types, including the Overman, on the other hand.[13]

With the death of the Christian god as background, *Zarathustra* begins with Zarathustra teaching the Overman as the new meaning of the earth. In the last speech of his prologue, Zarathustra warns that if humanity does not set the Overman as its goal and highest hope soon, then the coming of the "last man" will forever preclude the appearance of the Overman. "Alas, the time is coming when man will no longer shoot the arrow of his longing beyond man, and the string of his bow will have forgotten how to whir!"[14]

Zarathustra, however, is the story of Zarathustra's transformation from being merely a herald of the Overman to being the Overman himself. As part of his transformation, Zarathustra learns that the fundamental phenomenon of life is the will to power but philosophy – the most spiritual will to power – has hitherto been in the service of revenge. To be delivered from revenge, one must attain redemption, which Zarathustra defines as redeeming those who lived in the past and turning every "it was" into a "thus I willed it."[15] Zarathustra then applies the idea of the eternal recurrence to this new definition of redemption by willing the eternal recurrence of all things and thereby attains redemption.

By willing the eternal recurrence of all things, even of the smallest man, Zarathustra becomes the Overman, one who has overcome humanity, more specifically, his nausea of humanity. The word "Overman" designates Zarathustra's "supreme achievement" of attaining redemption through the willing of the eternal recurrence of all things. Thereafter, not only does Zarathustra embody the concept of the Overman, the supreme type of all beings, he is also the teacher of the eternal recurrence.

As the "fundamental conception" and "basic idea"[16] of *Zarathustra* as well as the "doctrine of Zarathustra,"[17] the idea of the eternal recurrence is more important than the better known concept of the Overman. Not only did Nietzsche solve the Yes-saying part of his task with the idea of the eternal recurrence, which he called the "highest formula of affirmation that is at all attainable,"[18] but Zarathustra's act of willing the eternal recurrence of all things is the foundational act of a new teaching that is liberated from the spirit of revenge and that is faithful to the earth.

With this foundational act of willing the eternal recurrence of all things, Zarathustra achieves a great victory over the "spirit of gravity," which represents Plato and all forms of Platonism, such as Christianity and its heir, the democratic enlightenment, that has hitherto been victorious in the centuries-long struggle between master morality and slave morality. At the end of the book, Zarathustra descends to humanity as a commander and legislator in order to implement the political consequences of his doctrine of the eternal recurrence and to bring about the Great Noon. These political consequences are Zarathustra's new values of a new nobility and its task of the higher breeding of humanity with the goal of human enhancement. The doctrine of the eternal recurrence is the foundational idea of the new era commencing at the Great Noon when humanity will be able to shoot the arrow of its longing beyond humanity.

Using similar archery imagery in *Beyond Good and Evil*, Nietzsche wrote that the "fight against Plato or [. . .] the fight against the Christian-ecclesiastical pressure of millennia [. . .] has created in Europe a magnificent tension of the spirit the like of which had never yet existed on earth: with so tense a bow we can now shoot for the most distant goals." Twice already attempts have been made to unbend the bow and release the tension that European man experiences as "need and distress." These attempts have been by means of Jesuitism and by means of the "democratic enlightenment." Nietzsche conceded that the latter might still succeed in unbending the bow. If the democratic enlightenment succeeds in releasing the tension of the taut bow of the modern spirit, then we shall no longer be able to shoot for the most distant goals but instead will degenerate into the "last man." Nevertheless, Nietzsche and other "*good Europeans* and free, *very* free spirits," who are "neither Jesuits nor democrats," still feel "the whole need of the spirit and the whole tension of its bow. And perhaps also the arrow, the task, and – who knows? – the *goal* –"[19]

These "*good Europeans* and free, *very* free spirits" are the "philosophers of the future" who complete the "revaluation of values" in order to achieve victory over the democratic movement – the latest form of Platonism – and to prevent the "degeneration and diminution of man into the perfect herd animal"[20] or, in Zarathustra's words, the "last man."[21] To avoid the last man, the task is the higher breeding of humanity and the goal is the "enhancement of the type 'man.'"[22] The means to this goal is a "good and healthy" nobility or aristocracy in an aristocratic society composed of a new European mixed race that has become "pure." Furthermore, Nietzsche wanted a unified Europe to experience his envisioned cultural rebirth during the new era and thought the best way to unify Europe was by the breeding of a new nobility that would rule Europe and the breeding of a new European race to eliminate the divisiveness of nationalism that prevents European unity.

The idea of the eternal recurrence is the foundational idea of the new era because this idea provides the basis of both the philosophy of the future and the religion of the future. This philosophy of the future, the new master morality, serves as the intellectual foundation of the new era. Yet, this new master morality is incomplete. Nietzsche predicted and called for the appearance of "philosophers of the future" to complete the creation of the new master morality and to establish a new nobility to tackle the greatest of all tasks, the higher breeding of humanity, with the goal of human enhancement. This nobility serves as the institutional foundation of the new era. The idea of the eternal recurrence also provides the basis of the religion of the future – the Dionysian faith – that the philosophers of the future will use in their project of human enhancement. Failing the appearance of these philosophers of the future, humanity will continue to degenerate into the "last man" and the possibility of a European cultural rebirth will end.

As "the last disciple of the philosopher Dionysus" and "the teacher of the eternal recurrence,"[23] Nietzsche is the herald of the new era that commences at the event called the Great Noon during which the project of human enhancement is consecrated. The Great Noon is also a religious event in which the Greek god Dionysus returns in his new incarnation created by Nietzsche. The Great Noon will then eventually usher in Hazar, Zarathustra's kingdom of a thousand years. This tragic age – the golden age of the new era – will be a period of European cultural rebirth in which tragedy, the highest art in saying Yes to life, will be reborn.

---

[1] A, Foreword.

[2] BGE, §285.

[3] Z I, On the Flies of the Market Place. "*Order of rank*: He who *determines* values and directs the will of millennia by giving direction to the highest natures is the *highest* man." WP, §999.

[4] GS, §1. "The most cautious friend of man will add: 'Not only laughter and gay wisdom but the tragic, too, with all its sublime unreason, belongs among the means and necessities of the preservation of the species.'" Ibid.

[5] Ibid.

[6] EH IV, §8.

[7] A, §62.

[8] GM I, §16.

[9] Ibid.

[10] EH-CW, §2.

[11] BGE, §228.

[12] Nietzsche, *Selected Letters*, 255.

[13] There is a similar dichotomy in *On the Genealogy of Morals* where Nietzsche

expressed "a sigh and a last hope." The sigh is "the diminution and leveling of European man" that "constitutes *our* greatest danger, for the sight of him makes us weary. [. . .] The sight of man now makes us weary – what is nihilism today if it is not *that*? – We are weary *of man*." The last hope is the "glance of something perfect, wholly achieved, happy, mighty, triumphant, something still capable of arousing fear! Of a man who justifies *man*, of a complementary and redeeming lucky hit on the part of man for the sake of which one may still *believe in man*!" GM I, §12.

[14] Z I, Prologue, §5.
[15] Z II, On Redemption.
[16] EH-Z, §1.
[17] EH-BT, §3.
[18] EH-Z, §1.
[19] BGE, Preface.
[20] BGE, §203.
[21] Z I, Prologue, §5.
[22] BGE, §257.
[23] TI X, §5.

FURTHER READING

If the reader is interested in reading Nietzsche's works but wants to focus on the ideas that are discussed in this book, I recommend the following selections to be read in the order specified.

Each subpart in *Ecce Homo* on Nietzsche's books should be read to obtain an insight into his own view of his book before the reader reads selections from that book for himself. Nietzsche's early books can be selectively read in chronological order: UM III, §§1, 5, and 6; HA I, §§25, 113, 246, and 247; HA II1, §§ 225 and 378; D, §§49, 103, 272, 563, and 571; and GS, §§ 1, 4, 19, 40, 73, 108, 109, 116, 125, 174, 259, 265, 267, 268, 269, 270, 271, 272, 273, 274, 275, 276, 277, 283, 290, 325, 340, 341, 342, 343, 362, 370, 377, and 382. When reading the sections from Book Five (Sections 343-382) of *The Gay Science*, keep in mind that they were written after the completion of *Thus Spoke Zarathustra* and *Beyond Good and Evil*.

Instead of reading *Thus Spoke Zarathustra* next (the book Nietzsche wrote after the first edition of *The Gay Science*), the following selections should be read in this order: BGE, Preface and §§42, 43, 44, 56, 61, 62, 195, 202, 203, 211, 212, 242, 251, 257, 258, 259, 260, 265, 285, 287, and 295; GM, Preface, §6; GM I, §§2, 5, 7, 10, 11, 12, 16, 17, and Note; GM II, §§16, 17, 24, and 25; GM III, §§14, 27, and 28; BT, Attempt at a Self-Criticism, §5; and CW, Epilogue.

Then each of the following books should be read in their entirety in this order: *Thus Spoke Zarathustra, Twilight of the Idols, The Anti-Christ,* and *Ecce Homo.*

SELECTED BIBLIOGRAPHY

Cate, Curtis. *Friedrich Nietzsche.* Woodstock, N.Y.: Overlook Press, 2002.

Gilman, Sander L., ed. *Conversations with Nietzsche: A Life in the Words of His Contemporaries.* Translated by David J. Parent. Oxford: Oxford University Press, 1987.

Lampert, Laurence. *Nietzsche's Task: An Interpretation of "Beyond Good and Evil."* New Haven: Yale University Press, 2001.

_____. *Nietzsche's Teaching: An Interpretation of "Thus Spoke Zarathustra."* New Haven: Yale University Press, 1986.

Nietzsche, Friedrich. *Beyond Good and Evil: Prelude to a Philosophy of the Future.* Translated by Walter Kaufmann. New York: Vintage Books, 1966.

_____. *The Birth of Tragedy* and *The Case of Wagner.* Translated by Walter Kaufmann. New York: Vintage Books, 1967.

_____. *Daybreak: Thoughts on the Prejudices of Morality.* Translated by R. J. Hollingdale. Cambridge: Cambridge University Press, 1982.

_____. *Dithyrambs of Dionysus.* Translated by R. J. Hollingdale. London: Anvil Press Poetry, 2001.

_____. *The Gay Science: With a Prelude in Rhymes and an Appendix of Songs.* Translated by Walter Kaufmann. New York: Vintage Books, 1974.

_____. *Human, All Too Human: A Book for Free Spirits.* Translated by R. J. Hollingdale. Cambridge: Cambridge University Press, 1986.

_____. *The Portable Nietzsche.* Edited and translated by Walter Kaufmann. New York: Penguin Books, 1976.

_____. *On the Genealogy of Morals* and *Ecce Homo.* Translated by Walter Kaufmann and R. J. Hollingdale. New York: Vintage Books, 1967.

_____. *Sämtliche Werke: Kritische Studienausgabe.* Edited by Giorgio Colli and Mazzino Montinari. Munich: de Gruyter, 1999.

_____. *Selected Letters of Friedrich Nietzsche.* Edited and translated by Christopher Middleton. Indianapolis: Hackett Publishing Company, 1996.

_____. *Thus Spoke Zarathustra: A Book for All and None.* Translated by Walter Kaufmann. New York: Penguin Books, 1978.

_____. *Twilight of the Idols* and *The Anti-Christ*. Translated by R. J. Hollingdale. Harmondsworth, U.K.: Penguin Books, 1968.

_____. *Untimely Meditations*. Translated by R. J. Hollingdale. Cambridge: Cambridge University Press, 1983.

_____. *The Will to Power*. Translated by Walter Kaufmann and R. J. Hollingdale. New York: Vintage Books, 1968.

_____. *Writings from the Late Notebooks*. Edited by Rüdiger Bittner. Translated by Kate Sturge. Cambridge: Cambridge University Press, 2003.

Richardson, John. *Nietzsche's New Darwinism*. Oxford: Oxford University Press, 2008.

Young, Julian. *Friedrich Nietzsche: A Philosophical Biography*. Cambridge: Cambridge University Press, 2010.

INDEX

(of Nietzsche's works quoted or cited herein with the note number(s) in parenthesis following the page number)

www.ingramcontent.com/pod-product-compliance
Lightning Source LLC
LaVergne TN
LVHW021448080426
835509LV00018B/2210